C000082483

GLYNDŴR'S FIRST VICTORY

Glyndŵr's
First Victory
The Battle of Hyddgen 1401

Ian Fleming

yLolfa

First edition: 2001

© Ian Fleming and Y Lolfa 2001

The text and pictures in this book are subject to copyright and may not be
reproduced by any means (except for review purposes) without the prior, written
consent of the publishers.

Cover design: Ceri Jones
Original painting: A.C. Michael

ISBN: 0 86243 590 0

Printed, published and bound in Wales
using acid-free and partly recycled paper
by Y Lolfa Cyf., Talybont, Ceredigion, SY24 5AP
e-mail ylolfa@ylolfa.com
internet www.ylolfa.com
phone (01970) 832 304
fax 832 782
isdn 832 813

CONTENTS

ACKNOWLEDGEMENTS

I would like to thank a number of people who both inspired me to investigate the topic of the Battle of Hyddgen and assisted with the research.

Tegwyn Griffiths of the Owain Glyndŵr Centre in Machynlleth really started me off on the project, as a result of a long conversation on a soaking wet day in mid June, when I dropped into the Centre during a backpacking trip! I would also like to thank Iorwerth Jones, formerly the Huntsman in the Hyddgen area. Henry Jones Davies of *Cambria* Magazine has been very supportive, as has Cledwyn Fychan who probably knows more about Hyddgen than anyone else alive.

The staff of the Royal Commission for Historical Monuments in Wales, Clwyd-Powys Archaeological Trust, Dyfed Archaeological Trust and the Owain Glyndŵr Society, have also been most helpful. The preparation of this book has involved visiting a host of often obscure (and sometimes strange) websites and has led me down numerous fascinating information byways, following up leads and checking data.

Most of all, I want to thank my wife Julia, who encouraged me to complete the project and not only patiently put up with many long explanations about mediaeval warfare and the topography of the Hyddgen area, but also read the draft of the text and made many helpful suggestions about improvements.

IAN FLEMING

The Battle of Hyddgen: Historical background

Hyddgen was a crucial battle. Until this Welsh victory in the Pumlumon foothills in the early summer of 1401, the Glyndŵr Revolt had been a sporadic and uncoordinated affair, with as many Welsh defeats as victories, demonstrating plenty of evidence of the repressive force of the English Crown. Although Owain Glyndŵr had been proclaimed Prince of Wales on 16 September 1400, he was, by the spring of 1401, a hunted outlaw, with his estates confiscated and only a handful of companions. The brilliant victory at Hyddgen showed that the Welsh rebels could defeat an organised, efficient force of soldiery. It provided the spark which rekindled the flames of revolt throughout Wales.

Hyddgen was a pivotal victory. All the subsequent events of the Glyndŵr Revolt flow from it; had Glyndŵr been defeated at Hyddgen it is probable that there would have been no deepening of the revolt. Glyndŵr, if he had managed to escape from the vengeful Anglo-Flemish troops, would have become a hunted outlaw once again and English royal power would have been reasserted in Wales over a decade early.

The start of the fifteenth century saw Wales in a state of discontent, which Owain Glyndŵr was able to capitalise on when he launched his revolt. For decades, there had been simmering resentment against English royal authority and Marcher rule, now exacerbated by the attempts of the new king, Henry IV, to exact heavy payments from his Welsh subjects. Although Richard II had been a capricious and autocratic monarch, his overthrow in 1399 by a tyrannical ruler of doubtful legality, Henry Bolingbroke, was not supported by the Welsh aristocracy. The new king was immediately menaced by war with the Scots, Irish and French and the start of his reign saw English royal commitments badly overstretched. The phrase much later used by Irish nationalist rebels – "England's difficulty is Ireland's opportunity"– could be taken, in 1400, to apply to Wales, if any leader of sufficient calibre came forward to take advantage of the situation. Such a leader was Owain Glyndŵr, a cultured aristocrat in his late 40s, with training in English law, experience of fighting for Richard II and links by blood to the old royal house of Powys. Glyndŵr's bitter dispute over land with Lord Grey of Ruthin provided the pretext for an armed rising, particularly as Grey had, by deception, given Henry IV the impression that Glyndŵr was a rebel even before he had risen in revolt.

One further factor deserves mention. In 1400, folk memories of the Edwardian conquest of Gwynedd in 1282 were still vivid. This was an era of prophecy. Travelling bards kept alive the ancient belief that the Welsh might one day drive out the Saxon invaders. Linguistic identity accentuated Welshness, as did the oppressive English laws imposed after the conquest.

Glanmor Williams, in his *Owain Glyndŵr* (1993), sums up a possible view of Owain Glyndŵr at the beginning of the fifteenth century:

> His earlier years of service to the Crown…together with his unique standing in Wales may have led him to expect appropriate patronage and recognition, which had not been forthcoming…To seal his discomfiture and reveal just how little his interests counted with Henry IV, had come the humiliating episode of his quarrel with Lord Grey of Ruthin. This could well have been the last straw; it was at this point that his awareness of Welshness, carefully nurtured by poets and, no doubt, by other followers…burst into flames. His

anger led him to cast aside all considerations of constraint and earlier loyalties.

On 16 September 1400, at Glyndyfrdwy, Owain Glyndŵr was proclaimed Prince of Wales by a group of relatives and friends including his brother, his eldest son, his brothers in law, the Dean of St Asaph and Crach Ffinnant, a "prophet". The proclamation was a defiant statement to Henry IV, who had already declared his son Prince Henry (the future Henry V) Prince of Wales, in the Edwardian Conquest tradition of so naming the eldest son of the English king. In his *Revolt of Owain Gyndŵr* (1997), Rees Davies comments:

> ...the very nature of the proclamation made it clear that this was a premeditated act based on long-festering grievances and an attachment to an ideology of an independent Wales governed by its own native, legitimate ruler. Such dreams are not suddenly manufactured in a moment of pique. It is also clear that the movement of 1400 was carefully planned and coordinated among the disaffected leaders of Welsh society in North Wales.

On 18 September, Glyndŵr and his followers (Plant Owain – Owain's Children) attacked, sacked and burnt Ruthin, the borough of Lord Grey, and then set about a devastating series of raids on the border castle towns, burning Flint, Rhuddlan, Holt, Hawarden, Denbigh, Oswestry and Welshpool. Lacking siege equipment, they were unable to attack the castles. Outside Welshpool on 24 September, they were met, on the banks of the Vyrnwy, by an English force under Sheriff Hugh Burnell, a professional soldier, with the levies of three English counties. Outnumbered, the Welsh rebel force of about 250 guerillas broke and scattered.

News of Glyndŵr's attacks reached Henry IV at Northampton and he sent out orders to call up men from ten English counties to organise a punitive expedition. By 26 September, the king was at Shrewsbury with a sizeable army. Meanwhile, rebellion was spreading in North Wales as Glyndŵr's cousins, Rhys and Gwilym Tudor, former protégés of Richard II, rose in Anglesey. Henry IV led his army on a rapid invasion of North Wales along the north coast, receiving submissions en route, although Rhys Tudor attacked the army near Beaumaris, forcing Henry IV to take refuge within the castle walls, and the king sacked Llanfaes Friary in retaliation.

Geoffrey Hodges in *Owain Glyndŵr and the War of Independence in the Welsh Borders* (1995) comments upon the strategy of the English:

> Riding through enemy territory and plundering had become known as chevauchée during the Hundred Years War…Wide, fair regions of France had been devastated by this crude medieval method of financing warfare…it was still worse for poor regions like Wales…where cattle and sheep represented the chief wealth of their owners…The looting of monasteries, churches, castles and farms could be profitable too; their destruction also satisfied the desire for vengeance and demoralised the enemy.

The English army completed a circuit of North Wales, via Caernarfon and Dinas Mawddwy, and by early October was back in Shrewsbury. Here, on 8 October, Owain Glyndŵr and other leading rebels were formally outlawed. The estates of Glyndŵr were confiscated and granted to the King's half brother, John Beaufort, Earl of Somerset. Glyndŵr himself withdrew into Snowdonia to a stronghold near Llyn Peris. It appeared, as winter drew on, that the rebellion had been stamped out.

The winter of 1400/01 offered Henry IV an ideal moment to deal intelligently with the grievances behind the revolt in the autumn, by showing clemency and understanding. He failed to take this opportunity and instead allowed himself to be swayed by the hysterical (and, using modern terminology, racist) views of the Parliament that met in January 1401. As Parliament passed repressive laws against the Welsh and the king imposed swingeing communal fines upon the rebel areas, Welsh labourers began to leave their work in England and Welsh students quit English universities, to return home and join Glyndŵr. Ian Skidmore, in his *Owain Glyndŵr Prince of Wales* (1996), makes the telling comment:

> ...in London, far away from the spears and the pillage, a more aggressive posture was being adopted by the Welsh in exile. To the exiled Welshman in London and at the universities in Oxford and Cambridge, to Welsh labourers who had come to England attracted by the well paid jobs that had become available since the Plague, the call of 'Hiraeth' was tantalising. Not for the last time in history, those furthest from the battle were the most eager that it should be joined.

Nevertheless, Glyndŵr's fortunes were at a low ebb in the winter and early spring of 1401. In March 1401, Henry IV felt secure enough to make an offer of a pardon to all rebels except Glyndŵr. Many submitted to the Crown and it is believed that Glyndŵr's following was reduced to a mere seven companions at one point. As the warmer spring weather came, however, the numbers of Owain's Children began to increase, partly as a result of the return of the exiles from England.

On 1 April 1401, the Tudor brothers captured Conwy Castle by a ruse when the garrison was at church, a success of staggering proportions in view of the size and strength of this Edwardian fortress. Although this strategem was bold and daring, the Tudors seem to have been motivated by a desire to force the Crown to grant them better terms for a possible pardon. This was eventually granted in June, after lengthy negotiations with Henry Percy ("Hotspur"), Justiciar of North Wales. The Conwy Castle episode was effectively a sideshow; the real business of revolt continued elsewhere, although with much less initial success. Rebel forces suffered two serious defeats during May. A band of Glyndŵr's men was routed by Hotspur near Cader Idris, and, falling back to Llyn Peris, was scattered by John Charlton, Lord of Powys. Charlton stated in a letter to Prince Henry, that he was *"on chevauchée with my men in the mountains of my country of Powys"* and Hotspur wrote, in a letter to the Privy Council:

> ...and please to know that news have reached me this day from the Sieur of Powys, as to his combat with Owen de Glyndyfrdwy, whom he hath discomfited, and wounded many of his men...

Charlton nearly captured Glyndŵr himself in the engagement (although it is just possible that the leader of the Welsh rebel band was not Glyndŵr himself, but his brother). He seized an ancient banner of mystical significance to the Welsh, together with some horses and lances, and one of Glyndŵr's henchmen. There is evidence that Charlton was well in control of the situation, with a band of reliable troops and a network of effective spies. All this indicates that Glyndŵr was sorely pressed in North Wales and it is possible that he had already decided to move his sphere of operations southwards when the defeats at the hands of Hotspur and Charlton occurred. Indeed, Charlton's letter to Prince Henry hints that the defeated rebels had fled southwards. Hotspur should really have pursued the advantage and followed immediately; there is good reason to believe that a decisive English response might have met with final success. However, Hotspur had become disillusioned with the whole business. His relations with the King were always strained and he was tired of financing his own military operations. Suddenly, he resigned his post and retired with a body of retainers to Scotland. In years to come, Henry IV would accuse Hotspur of making a secret treaty with Glyndŵr at this time. Certainly his departure took some of the pressure off the rebels in North Wales and probably contributed to the successes of Glyndŵr after the Battle of Hyddgen.

The precise chronology of events in April, May and June 1401 is almost impossible to establish. The whereabouts of Owain Glyndŵr at any point were shrouded in mystery; already he was beginning to gain a reputation as something of a magician. However, there was one indisputable and unpalatable fact for the Welsh rebels as May 1401 drew to a close. Although they had created destruction and mayhem as guerrillas and raiding parties, they had not, so far, won success on the field of battle, since they always melted away when faced by a disciplined English force.

It is likely that Glyndŵr had contemplated a move southwards for some time. Indeed, he might already have done so before the Hotspur and Charlton engagements. It was patently obvious that Glyndŵr's guerrillas were no match for organised Crown forces. There was too great a concentration of English forces in North Wales. The patient administration of Hotspur as Justiciar in the first part of the year, with his judicious granting of pardons where appropriate, had reconciled many former rebels, at least temporarily, to the re-establishment of Royal rule. Ian Skidmore comments:

> In the still peaceful south army garrisons were less vigilant and, unlike the north, there was no restriction on movement about the country. It was there that Owain decided to fight. Leaving a small party to defend his headquarters in Snowdonia, Owain moved his main force to a forward base on Plynlimmon Mountain in the central highlands of Wales, from which he could strike either into North Wales or into the rich lands of the South.

The highlands of Pumlumon were an ideal central base for Glyndŵr's rebel force. The area was well sited to receive reinforcements from North and South Wales and the remote valleys in the heart of the boggy uplands could be defended by a small but determined force with good local knowledge. The nature of the terrain made advance by an invading force difficult. Supplies for the rebels could be provided by sympathisers in the surrounding lowlands, particularly from the Dyfi Valley and the smaller fertile valleys encroaching upon the highlands in the north and west.

Sources for the period of Glyndŵr's sojourn in Pumlumon are almost non-existent, but it is likely that an advance party of rebels set up a base during May 1401 and that the main force, accompanied by Glyndŵr himself, moved south in the early part of June. Local tradition has placed Glyndŵr's base at Siambr Trawsfynydd, in the north of the Pumlumon massif and close to the wide marshy valley of the Afon Hyddgen; in the next section I will describe the topography of the area.

- Beaumaris
- Conwy Castle
- Flint
- Holt
- Hawarden
- Caernarfon Castle
- Denbigh
- Llyn Peris
- Ruthin
- Oswestry
- Cader Idris
- Welshpool
- Shrewsbury
- Machynlleth
- Montgomery
- PUMLUMON UPLANDS
- Rheidol
- Abbey Cwmhir
- New Radnor
- River Teifi
- Bishops Castle
- **Probable route of Anglo Flemish army June 1401**
- Hay
- Talgarth
- Carmarthen
- Abergavenny
- *Area of Anglo Flemish settlement*
- *Area of Anglo Flemish settlement*
- Grosmont
- Usk

PLACES ASSOCIATED WITH THE EARLY STAGES OF THE GLYNDŴR REVOLT 1400-1401

Modern England/Wales border

15

Pumlumon

A good starting point for a description of Pumlumon (usually Anglicised into Plynlimon) is to be found in the classic text *Geology and Scenery In England and Wales*, which describes the Central Wales plateau as follows:

> ...Central Wales appears as a monotonous plateau rising to nearly 2000 feet above sea level, stretching through Cardiganshire to north Pembrokeshire and Radnorshire. Lacking craggy mountains like those of the volcanic tracts, its hills are generally smooth in aspect...there are few crags and in many wide areas...few places showing bare rock; over vast stretches the uniformity of relief and colouring is remarkable.

> Plynlimon is the highest mountain in this tract and from its summit most of the essential features of the landscape can be seen. In fact, it is probably the best viewpoint in Wales...for much of the way to the summit, the path leads over poor pasture with patches of bog...there comes a point when, a few hundred feet from the summit, the whole expanse of the plateau becomes visible for miles to the south and east; the flat topped hills...seem to form a vast plain out of which Plynlimon raises its head.

But while Plynlimon may be one of the easiest mountains in Wales to ascend, its northern face has none of the gentleness of the other slopes, for beneath the summit a lake lies in the shelter of a deep cwm, from which rise steep grey cliffs:

> Here…ice erosion had led to the production of precipices in otherwise subdued country and these effects are most pronounced on the north facing slopes.

The Pumlumon tops are generally grassy, with little exposed rock, except on the northern face, and only small variations in height. The valleys between and around are very wide, shallow and treeless, with great expanses of windswept moor grasses and bog cotton. In grey, overcast conditions, the aspect is bleak and austere in the extreme. Many writers over the years have been contemptuous of the area and descriptions such as "shapeless mass" and "sodden weariness" have abounded. Thomas Pennant, on his travels in Wales, would not visit Pumlumon at all:

> I was dissuaded from making it a visit, being informed that it was an uninteresting object, the base most extensive, the top boggy and the view over a dreary and uninhabited country.

Gilpin came to Pumlumon in the early nineteenth century, in search of "the Picturesque" and was singularly unimpressed, stating:

> …there is not a sufficiency of water in the landscape to balance the land.

A mid-nineteeth century traveller, Peacock, was scathing, saying that anyone who ventured on the hill alone stood an excellent chance of never being seen again, having himself become lost amid black peaty bogholes. George Borrow was a little more positive in *Wild Wales* (1862), but his view of typical Pumlumon scenery was not enthusiastic:

> A mountainous wilderness extended on every side, a waste of russet coloured hills, with here and there a black craggy summit. No signs of life or cultivation were to be discovered and the eye might search in vain for a grove or even a single tree.

Pumlumon's main feature is a long gritstone ridge, rising slightly above the plateau of Central Wales to a height of 2,468 feet at Pumlumon Fawr. The other tops on the ridge, in descending order of height, are Pumlumon Arwystli (2,428'), Y Garn (2,244'), Pencerrigtewion (2,201'), Pumlumon Fach (2,192'), Carnfachbugeilyn (2,041') and Pumlumon Cwmbiga (2,008'). Not on the main ridge but forming part of the Pumlumon "massif" are the outlying tops of Foel Fadian (1,850') to the north east, and Carn or Mynydd Hyddgen (1,850') and Banc Llechwedd Mawr (1,837'), to the north.

The Pumlumon ridge marks the watershed between drainage westward to Cardigan Bay and eastward towards England and ultimately south to the Bristol Channel. The rivers Rheidol, Severn and Wye have their sources here; those of the Rheidol and Wye on the slopes of Pumlumon Fawr and that of the Severn two miles north-east, close to Carnfachbugeilyn. Other lesser rivers also rise in the Pumlumon uplands, including the Leri, flowing west and then north to Ynyslas at the mouth of the Dyfi; the Llyfnant, which flows westwards through a valley of great beauty to join the Dyfi near Glandyfi; the Dulas, going north and then west to the Dyfi east of Machynlleth; and the Twymyn, dropping through a spectacular gorge near Dylife and then flowing north to Llanbrynmair. Still smaller streams, like the Hengwm, feed these rivers.

To the south of the Pumlumon ridge, moorland foothills surround the route through the uplands that is today the A44 trunk road. To the north of the ridge, the high plateau continues towards the Dyfi valley. Almost due north of Pumlumon Fawr lies the Hyddgen Valley, the area best associated with Owain Glyndŵr.

The isolation of Pumlumon and the fact that this mountainous area gives birth to three of the most significant rivers in Wales has given the massif a special place in Welsh tradition and literature. Pumlumon has often been viewed as the third most important mountain in Wales. Clearly, on grounds of height or majesty of appearance, such a claim cannot be upheld, but the stature of Pumlumon Fawr on the Central

Wales plateau gives the mountain and ridge a special status. As George Borrow stated back in the 1860s:

> What…has more than anything else contributed to the celebrity of the hill is the circumstance of its giving birth to three rivers. The first of which, the Severn, is the principal stream in Britain; the second, the Wye, the most lovely river, probably, which the world can boast of; and the third, the Rheidol, entitled to high honour from its boldness and impetuosity, and the remarkable banks between which it flows on its very short course…

Lewis Glyn Cothi composed a pennillion in the fifteenth century referring to the three rivers of Pumlumon. This is an extract:

> From high Pumlumon's shaggy side
> Three streams in three directions glide
> To thousands at their mouths who tarry
> Honey gold and mead they carry

Pumlumon's high rainfall feeds the rivers and smaller streams flowing from the ridge and surrounding upland, and contributes to the boggy nature of much of the moorland. The area has a reputation for being wet or misty. This reputation is difficult to shed. Even the *Rough Guide to Wales* fosters it by commenting:

> Plynlimon is bleak and difficult walking…water oozes everywhere in this misty wilderness.

However, despite a reputation for rain, mist and boggy hazards to walking, the Pumlumon area can be a delight in clear, sunny weather. It is largely unaffected by the myriads of walkers that crowd the tops of Snowdonia or Cadair Idris; most of those seeking the top of Pumlumon Fawr do so by one of the easy routes up from the A44 and go no further along the Pumlumon Ridge or beyond, into the Hengwm and Hyddgen valleys.

The bare moorlands upon and around Pumlumon were, in medieval times, vast upland sheep walks, unencumbered by fences or woodlands. The medieval landscape has been altered by mining, forestry and, more recently, the construction of the Nant y Moch Reservoir. In the nineteenth century, mining for lead and other metals was begun and abandoned mines are to be found in several locations in and around the upland area. Since the First World War, large sections to the east (the huge Hafren Forest, to the west of Llyn Clywedog) and north and north-west of the Pumlumon massif, have been planted with conifers. The south-west upland area has been transformed by the construction of the Nant y Moch Reservoir. The reservoir was formed by damming the waters of the Rheidol, Hengwm and Llechwedd Mawr to produce an irregular crecent- shaped lake about 3 miles long. It took its name from a chapel which was drowned by the rising waters when the dam, 170 feet high and 1,150 feet long, was begun in 1965. The local scenery has since been softened a little by forestry plantations along the western side of the reservoir, while, after several decades, the lake fits more naturally into the landscape.

Pumlumon has never seen much permanent human habitation. The uplands remain an area of wilderness with few signs of human activity, other than the shearing sheds in the Hyddgen Valley and at Bugeilyn. Former farms and cottages at Bugeilyn, in the lower Hengwm valley and at the confluence of Hyddgen and Hengwm, are now ruined and deserted. Pumlumon (Plynlimon) is now a rural Crown estate, 1,202 hectares (2,970 acres) in extent, mainly given over to sheep farming on a large scale. There is an important nature reserve in the north of the upland area around Glaslyn, protecting some of the best heather moorland in Wales.

Hyddgen

Tradition has associated Owain Glyndŵr with Pumlumon, but it is with the Hyddgen area, rather than with Pumlumon Fawr, that the principal activities of the Welsh rebels during the summer of 1401 have been linked. There are isolated (and possibly misleading) accounts of Glyndŵr riding to the summit of Pumlumon, unfurling his golden dragon banner, encamping there and leaving a hoof print of his horse at Craig y March. My belief is that the term "Pumlumon" might have been used in a rather loose sense and that mention of Glyndŵr on Pumlumon might refer to his activities *in the Pumlumon uplands*, rather than necessarily upon the crowning peak, Pumlumon Fawr.

At this point it seems appropriate to provide a description of the Hyddgen valley. The only written sources for the Battle of Hyddgen take us clearly into this area, while local oral traditions also point to Hyddgen, together with Siambr Trawsfynydd. The Hyddgen valley itself has probably changed remarkably little over the 600 years since Glyndŵr was active here, but forestry has brought considerable change to the north of Hyddgen, especially to the Siambr Trawsfynydd, where tradition has Glyndŵr's force encamped prior to the Battle of Hyddgen.

The Hyddgen valley is a wide, treeless and bleak tract of marshy lowland, drained by the Afon Hyddgen. At its southern end it joins the valley of the Afon Hengwm, which has run broadly south-westerly from Bugeilyn along the bottom of the Pumlumon Ridge. The Hengwm valley is another wide featureless tract, with one ill–defined path traversing boggy moorland grass and almost no trees to relieve the monotony, although a small clump is to be found near the Hyddgen/ Hengwm confluence. There are two ruined cottages in the lower part of the Hengwm valley. This must have been a particularly desolate spot in which to live.

The Hyddgen joins the larger Hengwm a short way downstream from where the infant Rheidol joins the Hengwm, flowing down (as Nant y Llyn) from the lake beneath Pumlumon Fawr's northern crags. Less than a mile downstream, the combined rivers Rheidol, Hengwm and Hyddgen enter the dark expanse of Nant y Moch reservoir. To view the area as it would have appeared in medieval times, a leap of imagination is required is to eliminate the Nant y Moch reservoir. Picture instead the Rheidol flowing south-west in a deeply incised valley joined by the Afon Llechwedd Mawr as it flowed past Drosgol and then turning south by Bryn Gwyn to flow towards Ponterwyd on its present course.

Where the Hyddgen joins the Hengwm, both rivers are fast flowing and not easily fordable. At its southern end the Hydggen valley narrows to a couple of hundred yards, with Banc Llechwedd Mawr on the west and Banc Lluestnewydd on the east sloping down to the river. On the west bank of the Hyddgen at this point are the so-called Covenant Stones of Owain Glyndŵr, on a comparatively flat grassy shelf above the river. This has, for some, been a tempting spot to imagine as the site of the Battle of Hyddgen, but my belief is that the conflict did not take place here.

A little further north, the Hyddgen valley opens out into a wide, flat, boggy area. The Afon Hyddgen is fed by a number of small streams flowing down from the high land to the east. Banc Lluestnewydd is the southern extension of an area of high moorland that reaches its highest point at Carn Hyddgen, or Mynydd Hyddgen. Here, at an altitude of 1,850 feet, is a superb viewpoint, topped by two immense stone cairns, which are marked as Carn Gwilym on the OS map. The hilltop is a small flat plateau, dropping sharply on all sides. To the north-east of Mynydd Hyddgen, a bleak landscape of peat bogs and moorland grass extends towards Bugeilyn, two miles distant.

The Hyddgen valley is at its widest point just below Mynydd Hyddgen, where the Nant y Garn flows down the north-west side of the hill, joining the Afon Hyddgen near a curious rocky knoll on the east of the valley. Near here, the modern shearing sheds stand alongside the river, where the track down from Bryn Moel crosses it on a simple bridge. There is an air of desolation and melancholy about this valley. One story has it haunted by the ghosts of a shepherd and his wife, she perpetually seeking her lost husband by the light of a lantern wavering along the hillside.

The Afon Hyddgen at the shearing sheds is only just over a mile from the confluence with the Hengwm but the river technically begins its brief life here, for a number of smaller streams combine, at or near this point, to form the river from which the valley takes its name. The Nant Bryn Moel rises on the southern slopes of its namesake hill and flows east to join the Hyddgen; the Nant Goch, fed by the Nant Goch Fach, flows south-east from the slopes of Mynydd Bychan, which closes off the northern end of the Hyddgen valley. Finally, the Llygnant flows south-east towards Hyddgen and forms an extension of the valley between the peaty hillside of Ochr Llygnant and the slopes of Esgair y Ffordd to the north. Here another leap of the imagination is called for to visualise the medieval landscape, since forestry today covers the whole of Mynydd Bychan and Esgair y Ffordd and forestry activities have altered the appearance of the Siambr Trawsfynydd, which lies north-east of Esgair y Ffordd. Indeed, a huge area of coniferous plantations now extends northwards beyond Mynydd Bychan, down the deep valley of the Hengwm (a different Hengwm from the one mentioned earlier), past the lofty cliffs of Creigiau Bwlch Hyddgen and on to Talbontdrain.

At the time of the Battle of Hyddgen, the whole of this area, now so heavily forested with conifers, was likely to have been treeless, or, just possibly, some of the hillsides may have been partly cloaked with ancient oakwoods. It is quite likely, however, that the hills would have been similar in appearance to the Hyddgen valley and the hills to its east and west as they are today. Picture, then, the northern end of the Hyddgen valley, not hemmed in by a green line of forestry plantations, but crowned by the bare hill of Mynydd Bychan (around 1,300 feet), perhaps dotted with some isolated clumps of woodland, and, to the east of this eminence, the grassy ridge of Esgair y Ffordd, rising to about 1,200 feet. Beyond Esgair y Ffordd lay a deep valley cut by a small stream which flowed down from the high land at the northern edge of the Pumlumon upland. Here was a rocky cleft in the hillside, Siambr Trawsfynydd, opening out below into areas of flat land beside the stream, perhaps with occasional clumps of scrubby undergrowth, where a semi-permanent camp could be set up in relative safety.

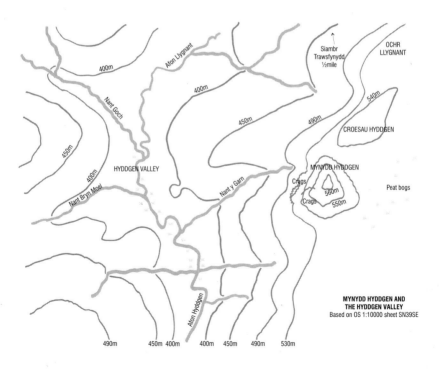

**MYNYDD HYDDGEN AND
THE HYDDGEN VALLEY**
Based on OS 1:10000 sheet SN39SE

Glyndŵr in Pumlumon

Glyndŵr's followers came to Pumlumon during the early summer of 1401, probably from May onwards. It is likely that an advance party set up a permanent camp and that Glyndŵr himself joined them slightly later. Defeats at the hands of Hotspur and Charlton had temporarily made North Wales a dangerous area, although, as already noted, Hotspur quitted his post of Justiciar and left for Scotland just as the rebels were moving south.

The only written source for Glyndŵr's move to the Pumlumon uplands is the Peniarth MS, *The Annals of Owen Glyn Dwr*, written by Gruffydd Hiraethog between 1556 and 1564, but believed to have been based upon a early fifteenth century manuscript. The text is spare indeed:

> The following summer Owen arose with 120 reckless men and robbers and he brought them in warlike fashion to the uplands of Ceredigion...

Some later writers added a little to this basic account. Thomas Ellis, in *Memoirs of Owen Glendowr* in 1775, claimed to have had access to other early sources. His account states that, having arrived in the Pumlumon area, Glyndŵr:

> ...thence did much hurt, sending parties to pillage the country round about.

We can envisage small raiding parties from the uplands descending upon Mid and South Wales, both areas hitherto largely untouched by the rebellion. It seems that this activity was already under way during May, even before Charlton's victory over Glyndŵr, since there is evidence that Parliament was becoming increasingly jittery about the rebel activity in South Wales:

> Owain Glyndŵr and others have newly made insurrection and have gathered together in the marches of Carmarthenshire.
> They conspire to invade the realm and destroy the English.

Panic talk indeed, since the rebel activities still consisted of sporadic and opportunist raids, but the legend of Owain Glyndŵr was already growing in the minds of the English legislators. Glyndŵr met the highly influential Henry Dwn of Cydweli Castle in Carmarthenshire at this time and the support of this former member of Richard II's retinue was obtained for the rebel cause. This is evidence of a considerable southward extension of the revolt, which had hitherto been very much a North Wales affair.

A detailed, although possibly slightly suspect, account of Glyndŵr's movements at this time is to be found in Archaeologia Cambrensis of 1851. Ascribed to a Mr T O Morgan, the extract entitled *Historical and Traditional Notices of Owain Glyndŵr* details the raids launched from Glyndŵr's Pumlumon base of operations, and provides a lengthy description of the Battle of Hyddgen (often embellished with Victorian persiflage). The Archaeologia Cambrensis account may have drawn upon earlier sources, now lost, but there is also the possibility of a certain amount of "historical embroidery". Since there is such a paucity of source material for the topic, it is worth drawing upon the account, although caution is appropriate.

The *Archaeologia Cambrensis* extract states:

> As Owain's influence and interest lay both in North Wales and in South Wales, during the summer of 1401 he marched with a detachment of his army, consisting of one hundred and twenty men at arms, and posted them on Plynlimon, on the confines

of Cardiganshire and Montgomeryshire. The selection of this position by Owain as the basis of his future operations, offensive and defensive, evinced great foresight and policy, as from its central position it was admirably adapted for receiving succours from his vassals and friends in each part of the Principality. His small band of men, entrenched by the numerous and extensive turbaries which surround it, and are only passable at certain points, might have braved the whole power of his invaders for a long time, if supplied with provisions. The position was also well suited for the purpose of hostile excursions into the Marches...

There is an interesting footnote about the definition of the term "man-at-arms". According to a French medieval authority quoted by Pennant, one "man-at-arms" consisted of three archers and a swordsman, which would mean that Glyndŵr's force in the Pumlumon area numbered 480 individuals, all foot soldiers. Doubtless the distinction between archers and swordsman was a meaningless one in the context of raiding and the kind of irregular operations which the Welsh rebels had been mainly engaged in to date.

Before considering the location of the rebel camp, it is appropriate to review Glyndŵr's raiding activities in the summer of 1401. It is impossible to be certain which raids took place before the Battle of Hyddgen and which after. Many recent writers on the Glyndŵr Revolt have taken the view that the major incursions, such as the sacking of New Radnor and the destruction of Abbey Cwmhir, occurred after the battle. For example, Skidmore, in *Owain Glyndŵr, Prince of Wales*, comments:

> The path of Owain's Children after [the battle] was marked in fire...At Radnor, Owain sacked the castle and beheaded the entire garrison of sixty in the outer ward. Cistercian monks fled as Owain's rebels burned down the Abbey of Cymer, in revenge...for the Abbot's submission to Henry. Montgomery

town was left a smouldering ruin, its streets choked with dead...

The *Archaeologia Cambrensis* account, on the other hand, sees such major raids as precursors to the Battle of Hyddgen, stating that, in the early summer of 1401, Glyndŵr:

> ...ravaged such parts of the county of Montgomery as proved hostile; the county town of Montgomery was taken by surprise and sacked; the suburbs of Pool [Welshpool] were burnt; the Abbey of Cwmhir also felt his power. He next visited Maelienydd, or New Radnor, a place at that time of great strength, being fortified by the Lords marcher with a wall and castle. The garrison, consisting of threescore men, were all brought out and beheaded on the brink of the castle yard, and the town laid in ashes; and it has never recovered its former importance since that desolating visitation.

As with the chronology of events in the early months of 1401, it is now impossible to state with authority that these raids were pre- or post-Hyddgen. The truth is probably that certain raids occurred before the battle and others after. The sacking of Montgomery and Abbey Cwmhir seem more like opportunist guerrilla operations than the substantial descent upon New Radnor and the attack on Welshpool. Perhaps they occurred before Hyddgen was won, and Glyndŵr's offensive capability had been augmented.

A more telling account in the *Archaeologia Cambrensis* extract draws attention to Glyndŵr's operations in the south:

> This list of military operations planned here might be much augmented, as the castle of Dinas, near Talgarth, was burnt, and those of Hay, Abergavenny, Grosmont, Usk, Bishops Castle and others, were all, either in part or wholly, the victims of his daring sallies.

The revolt was now being carried to the far south and south-east of

Wales, with attacks upon substantial strongholds. There is mention of burning the castle at Talgarth, lying on the north-west extremity of the Black Mountains and guarding the pass towards Crickhowell and Abergavenny, but the other castles noted were probably attacked with less complete success, although outlying settlements and farms were undoubtedly destroyed in the process. The Welsh rebel bands still lacked the capacity for siege warfare. This is an impressive list of raids, however, for a rebel leader so recently at the point of defeat in North Wales.

Of even more immediate significance to the fortunes of Owain Glyndŵr was his operation in south-west Wales. His raids from the Pumlumon base into Cardiganshire and beyond into Pembrokeshire stirred up a substantial response from the Anglo-Flemish community in Southern Pembrokeshire:

> Owain, perceiving the fidelity and attachment of the Flemish inhabitants of Pembrokeshire and the lower part of Cardiganshire to the interest of the English king, made them also feel his presence by incursions upon them from his stronghold of Plynlimon. These Flemings were the descendants of that people who had been planted as a colony by Henry I at Rhoose [Rhos] in Pembrokeshire to curb and harass the native Welsh. And Glyndŵr in turn now...harassed them.

The Flemish colonists of southern Pembrokeshire had come as mercenary troops for the early Plantagenet kings and, in an early "plantation", had driven the native Welsh out of the area, so creating the settlement which later became known as "Little England Beyond Wales". This twelfth century ethnic cleansing had been carried out with ruthless efficiency, so that the native Welsh were forced north into the less fertile lands of northern Pembrokeshire. A clear distinction was soon evident between the "Englishry" to the south and the "Welshry" to the north. Today, the absence of Welsh placenames in south Pembrokeshire testifies to the completeness of the ethnic and linguistic displacement carried out by the Flemish colony. Since the early twelfth century, Flemish and Anglo-Flemish settlers had pushed east and north, into the Gower and into the fertile lands of southern Cardiganshire. These people owed their success as colonists and their modest prosperity to the support and patronage of the English Crown and so the activities of Glyndŵr in the summer of 1401 would have represented to them a considerable threat.

Thomas Ellis's account states:

> The Flemings of Rhos, Pembroke and Cardigan, whom
> Owain distressed most of all, raised 1500 men and went against
> him, being full of confidence that they would either kill or take
> him.

No details have survived about the nature of Owain Glyndŵr's raids into south-west Wales, but we can envisage rebel guerrillas descending from the hills, attacking and burning isolated farms and driving off cattle and sheep. The operations in this part of Wales did not strike at castles or towns, but, by raiding the prosperous holdings of the Anglo-Flemish settlers, perhaps even as far south as southern Pembrokeshire, Glyndŵr so enraged them that they determined to retaliate.

Let us take stock for a moment and draw a picture of the rebel operations and successes towards the end of June 1401. We can envisage Glyndŵr secure in his Pumlumon base, with his band of around 500, probably augmented by additional supporters, drawn by the stories of raiding successes and the lure of loot. Rebel bands operated towards the east and north-east, sacking Montgomery and Abbey Cwmhir; towards the south-east, with daring raids upon castles in and around the Black Mountains and in the Marches; and towards the south-west, where the secure prosperity of the Anglo-Flemish community was severely threatened by the depradations of the rebels. Returning warbands drove before them captured sheep and cattle, together with hostages and plundered items from farms and settlements. Some of the valleys in the Pumlumon uplands began to fill with stolen flocks and herds. We can imagine that life in the rebel camp was good, as news was received of an almost continual stream of rebel successes.

So where was Glyndŵr's summer base in the Pumlumon area? Gruffydd Hiraethog is of little help, since he referred only to "the uplands of Ceredigion". Some commentators have suggested that Glyndŵr camped actually on Pumlumon (presumably Pumlumon Fawr) despite the fact that such a location would be highly inappropriate, with no shelter, difficult access on the northern side and generally unpredictable weather conditions. Of course, one of the myths about Owain Glyndŵr, from the English side, certainly after 1401, was that he could somehow control the weather, but the idea of a rebel camp on Pumlumon Fawr stretches credulity too far. It is likely that a rebel outpost was maintained on the peak, to provide advance warning of the approach of an enemy. A medieval spearhead, found near the summit, may have been from this period. Furthermore, there are, as already noted, several suggestions that Glyndŵr raised his standard on Pumlumon, but I suspect that the term "Pumlumon" may here mean the whole upland area.

Chris Barber, in *In Search of Owain Glyndŵr* (1998), suggests that the rebel camp may have been west of Pumlumon in the area now covered by the Nant y Moch reservoir. He states that "entrenchments, spearheads and weapons have been found there over the years", but a search of the records in the Royal Commission for Historical Monuments in Wales and of the Clwyd-Powys Archaeological Trust, has failed to confirm this.

Since the Battle of Hyddgen has been recorded by one reasonably authentic written source (Gruffydd Hiraethog's account), most recent writers have sidestepped the issue of a base camp by suggesting that the battle took place in the Hyddgen valley and that the Anglo-Flemish force descended unexpectedly upon Glyndŵr's men camped there. I will examine different views of the battle location in the next section. The idea of a camp in the Hyddgen valley has always seemed an implausible one, since the valley is broad and marshy (it probably was very similar in 1401), with little or no shelter or protection. Written sources have been of very limited value so far on this; they fail to record anything at all about Glyndŵr's base, except that it was in the Pumlumon area. I will turn to oral tradition to locate a base for a substantial body of armed men (at least 500 and possibly many more at times), together with retainers, camp followers, hostages and prisoners, pack animals, horses and supplies for a sustained and lengthy campaign of guerilla warfare.

Cledwyn Fychan, who has been studying for many years the oral traditions of the Hyddgen shepherds, believes that Glyndŵr's base was at Siambr Trawsfynydd, slightly north-east of the Hyddgen valley. Oral tradition is very important in Wales and, in an area like the Pumlumon uplands, there has been little migration of local rural families over the centuries, so that stories passed down from father to children are distorted relatively little in the telling. The identification of Siambr Trawsfynydd may only be attributable to oral tradition, some might even call it legend, but such tradition should not be scorned simply because we have no written evidence to support it.

Siambr Trawsfynydd has changed radically since 1401. If you visit the site today, the view is of conifer plantations not bare moorland. The Forestry Commission constructed a forest road several years ago that has largely obliterated the Siambr. In the fifteenth century, however, there really was a Siambr (Chamber) at this spot, a large cleft in the hillside which provided protection for a small group of men. The rock is relatively soft and easily eroded. Slightly further west, there was flat land beside the stream flowing through the Siambr which could have been used by many of Glyndŵr's followers. All that is visible today is some marshy flat land alongside the stream, amid scrub and small trees.

Cledwyn Fychan believes that Glyndŵr stabled his horses in a cave (Y Stablau) further north in the isolated valley which drops down from the gorge of Tarren Gesail towards Aberhosan. He also noted that Rhosygarreg, in the same valley, was a grange of Strata Marcella Abbey and that Glyndŵr may have received support from the monks responsible for this upland sheepwalk. The tradition of horses being stabled in a cave near Rhosygarreg, as well as that of Siambr Trawsfynydd itself, has also been recounted by Iowerth Jones, former huntsman in the Hyddgen area. There is another story concerning Glyndŵr's horses useing makeshift rocky stabling under the crags of Creigiau Bwlch Hyddgen.

Elissa Henken, in *National Redeemer: Owain Glyndŵr in Welsh Tradition* (1996), comments that oral tradition is very significant. One reference to the Siambr Trawsfynydd tradition which she has recorded is worth noting:

> The following information…was collected in the 1960s from a Mr Pugh, concerning Siambr Trawsfynydd, a cleft in the rock near Hyddgen…

> …he heard from his father that that was where Owain Glyndŵr's soldiers slept when the English came at their worst upon them and that many of them were buried on the mountain nearby. Mr Pugh said that the old people used to tell this story as if they truly believed it and not like some of the other traditions.

What are we to conclude about the location and nature of Glyndŵr's summer base? Common sense surely dictated a sheltered and well concealed site, relatively accessible for supply from the lowlands to the north, and roomy enough to accommodate all or most of Glyndŵr's men, together with the camp followers and retainers already mentioned. Siambr Trawsfynydd certainly offered shelter of a limited kind, some protection from the prevailing south-westerly winds, and easy access to the lowlands, via the Afon Hengwm and also down Cwm Gwarchiau toward Aberhosan. We cannot state conclusively that Glyndŵr used the Siambr as a permanent base throughout the time he was in the Pumlumon area, but the likelihood is strong. Certainly, given the very nature of guerilla warfare and the tradition of chevauchée, now increasingly practised by the Welsh rebels, it is likely that, at any time, a proportion of Glyndŵr's force would have been away from base. Equally, outposts were probably maintained throughout the Pumlumon uplands, although these may have been manned by only two or three men at most. Pumlumon Fawr must have had such a post; possibly other Pumlumon summits to the north-east may have done so, and I suspect that Mynydd Hyddgen must also have seen a small detachment of men, ready to provide advance warning of any invasion of the uplands by the forces of the Crown.

Sources of information about the Battle of Hyddgen

Mention has already been made of the paucity of written sources of information about the events of the summer of 1401 and, more particularly, about the Battle of Hyddgen itself. There is almost nothing in the way of primary sources which can be used. The main source is by Gruffydd Hiraethog, written between 1556 and 1564, and believed to be based on a manuscript of 1422 which provided a history of Wales up to that date. Gruffydd Hiraethog essentially copied the earlier account, and his version, as the *Annals of Owen Glyn Dwr*, survives as the Peniarth MS 135 in the National Library.

If we can, by stretching the point, call Gruffydd Hiraethog's account a primary source, we must now move on to consider secondary sources. Some of these, over the next 300 years, may have also drawn upon primary sources which are now lost. A variety of Welsh men of letters used the fifteenth century manuscript, plus Hiraethog's version, as the basis for their histories. In the seventeenth century, Robert Vaughan of Hengwrt issued an account of the Glyndŵr Revolt, *The History of Ywein Glyndŵr*, using both the earlier source material and local traditions from Merioneth. It is likely that Thomas Ellis, probably an associate or friend of Vaughan, also drew upon such sources for his *Memoirs of Owain Glendowr*, which eventually appeared in 1775. It is also possible that Thomas Pennant, in the first part of *Tours in Wales* (1778), used both early manuscript material and these later accounts when he wrote his history of the Glyndŵr revolt.

In the nineteenth century, William Owen of Beaumaris produced a pamphlet *Hanes Owain Glandwr* (1833), which appears to have drawn largely upon Pennant. J E Lloyd, who wrote in 1931 the definitive account *Owen Glendower*, which is still regarded as a classic, believed that William Owen may have had access to some other early source material. However, his pamphlet was too slim to do more than mention Hyddgen.

A final source which appears to have used earlier material, and which addresses the Battle of Hyddgen in some detail, is the account *Historical and Traditional Notices of Owain Glyndŵr*, in Archaeologia Cambrensis (1851). It is not clear how much of this account, written by T O Morgan, is based upon original sources (although the text does appear to extend the description of the battle provided by Thomas Ellis) and how much can be ascribed to early Victorian embellishment. Since it contains so much detail about the build-up to Hyddgen and the battle itself, we cannot ignore it. It appears that Murray Urquhart, who painted (in 1909) the "Battle of Hyddgen" mural in the Owain Glyndŵr Centre in Machynlleth, was influenced by the Archaeologia Cambrensis account of the battle.

Most of the modern accounts of the Glyndŵr Revolt make some mention of the Battle of Hyddgen, but the accounts of the location and nature of the battle vary greatly. With the exception of the classic J E Lloyd text *Owen Glendower* which appeared in 1931, most of the modern texts were published very late in the century. Skidmore's *Owain Glyndŵr, Prince of Wales* first appeared in 1978 and several accounts were then published in the 1990s: Glanmor Williams's *Owain Glyndŵr* in 1993, Hodges' *Owain Glyndŵr and the War of Independence in the Welsh Borders* in 1995, Davies's *Revolt of Owain Glyndŵr* in 1995, Henken's *National Redeemer: Owain Glyndŵr in Welsh Tradition* in 1996, Barber's *In Search of Owain Glyndŵr* in 1998.

The Glyndŵr Revolt is also covered in a large number of other texts about Welsh history. The Battle of Hyddgen often gets a mention and is usually credited as a significant event.

Accounts of the Battle of Hyddgen

From the previous section, we can see that there is little detailed description of the battle, except in the *Archaeologia Cambrensis* account of 1851. This section provides an overview of the descriptive accounts from the early source material and demonstrates the contradictory ways modern writers have dealt with the battle.

Gruffydd Hiraethog's description of the battle is simple:

> The following summer Owen arose with 120 reckless men and robbers and he brought them in warlike fashion to the uplands of Ceredigion; and 1,500 men of the lowlands of Ceredigion and of Rhos and Penfro assembled there and came to the mountain with the intent to seize Owen. The encounter was on Hyddgant Mountain, and no sooner did the English troops turn their backs in flight than 200 of them were slain.

There is no doubt about the location of the battle from this account; Gruffydd Hiraethog states firmly that it was 'on Hyddgant Mountain', which we can, I suggest, take to mean Mynydd Hyddgen.

Thomas Ellis's embellished account gives a little more detail:

> ...They hemmed him in on all sides at a place called Mynyddhyddgant, so that he could not possibly get off without fighting at a great disadvantage. He and his men fought manfully a great while, in their own defence, against them. Finding themselves surrounded and hard put to it, they resolved at length to fight their way through or perish in the

attempt; so falling on furiously with courage whetted by despair, they put the enemy, after sharp dispute, to confusion; and they pursued so eagerly their advantage that they made them give ground, and in the end to fly outright, leaving two hundred of their men on the spot of engagement.

Ellis is a little less specific about the location of the battle; although identifying Mynydd Hyddgen, he does not clearly state that the engagement took place on the mountain. However, his use of the term "could not possibly get off" implies a hilltop location.

And so to the *Archaeologia Cambrensis* account, by T O Morgan, of 1851. It does seem that this account drew on the earlier Gruffydd Hiraethog and Thomas Ellis manuscripts, but there is a substantial amount of additional material and detail, which could indicate that the author had access to some other sources. We should have reservations about the accuracy of the *Archaeologia Cambrensis* account, but it cannot be ignored.

> And Glyndŵr in turn now so harassed them [the inhabitants of Pembrokeshire and South Cardiganshire] that, bent on retaliation and the removal of so dangerous an enemy, they assembled a body of fifteen hundred men, made a most expeditious march, and such was the celerity of their movements, that they succeeded in detaching Glyndŵr from his main position on Plynlimon, and surrounded him and his men on a neighbouring mountain called Mynydd Hyddgen, to great disadvantage.

There is a slightly confusing statement about Glyndŵr being based "on Plynlimon", which I have already suggested could be taken to mean the Pumlumon upland area generally, but this account specifically claims Mynydd Hyddgen as the location of the battle and indicates that the invading force moved so rapidly that it was able to lay siege to the hilltop.

A lengthy footnote in Archaeologia Cambrensis comments upon

the location in much more detail:

> Hyddgen, the scene of action, is an upland farm or sheep walk
> in Montgomeryshire, and lies north from Plynlimon somewhat
> more than three miles, and is separated from that mountain by
> the river Rheidol and its channel. The top of Hyddgen, called
> Y'r Wylfa, or the Watch Tower, very characteristically, from
> the view it affords of the early channel of the Rheidol, and of
> the hills on each side, presents a circular area of firm ground,
> surrounded by a sharp declivity or sloping front, while the
> ground below is soft and yielding. The position, therefore, was
> one that might be tenable for a long time, by a force of
> determination and spirit, against another much superior in
> number, if not forced to surrender for want of supplies.

The battle itself is now described as follows:

> Here Owain and his chosen band, which could not have
> exceeded 500 men, were encompassed on all sides of the hill
> by the superior number of his opponents, thirsting for revenge
> and eager for the fray. Like the lion taken in the toils, he made
> a long, vigorous and obstinate resistance; but when he found it
> impossible to retain his position any longer, cut off from all
> supplies, and that he had no alternative than to surrender or
> make some desperate effort, he addressed his followers with a
> fervour excited by the occasion, telling them that they must be
> prepared to die of famine, or cut their way through the enemy
> sword in hand; as if unsuccessful, there was nothing to
> anticipate but death. Finally, he urged them, if death were to
> be their doom, at least to meet it with arms in their hands.
> Upon this, he directed them to charge the enemy, and give no
> quarter; and they executed the command with such
> impetuosity, that the Flemings, thrown into confusion, took to
> flight in the greatest disorder, leaving 200 of their party dead
> on the field of battle.

This account describes an engagement begun by the Anglo-Flemish force surrounding the hilltop. An initial sharp skirmish in which the invaders were perhaps repulsed easily, since the Welsh force held the advantage of high ground, was followed by a lengthy period when the hilltop was encircled and the defenders suffered constant attacks from different directions, as well as flights of arrows aimed high to pick off random members of Glyndŵr's band. The Anglo-Flemish force could afford to wait until the defenders grew weak from lack of supplies. If Glyndŵr had been forced to establish the defensive position at short notice, food and perhaps water could have run out in a few days. (There are marshy pools near the summit of Mynydd Hyddgen, which could have provided a limited water supply.) Glyndŵr's appeal to his men to sell their lives dearly makes a lot of sense in the context of a besieged force running out of food, weakened by constant skirmishes, and denied reinforcement. Glyndŵr's victory over the Anglo-Flemish troops was therefore all the more remarkable. The Welsh force flung themselves on the besieging troops and fought with a desperation borne of the knowledge that they really had no alternative. Perhaps the besiegers had grown slack and over-confident; perhaps they believed that it was only a matter of time before Glyndŵr would be forced to seek terms; in any event, the sudden downward rush of the Welsh caught them off guard and they broke and ran.

Moving to slightly more modern accounts of the battle, we find another which appears to confirm a hilltop location, *Owen Glyndŵr* by A G Bradley (1928):

> The Flemings…of South Pembrokeshire and the Carmarthen littoral now marched against Owen 1,500 strong and engaged him on a spur of Plynlimon. Outnumbered and surrounded, the Welsh leader only escaped by cutting his way through his enemies, leaving 200 of them dead on the mountain.

The Mynydd Hyddgen location is confirmed in another account, *The Cistercian Abbey of Cwmhir* by S W Williams (1890):

Owen Glyndŵr, having encamped with his army at Mynydd Hyddgant on Plynlimon mountain in 1401, from thence sent out predatory expeditions against the English settlers in Wales.

From the 1930s onwards, the location of the Battle of Hyddgen was dealt with in a much more cavalier and less accurate manner. J E Lloyd's classic *Owen Glendower* (1931), despite including the text of Gruffydd Hiraethog's account in its appendices, describes the battle as follows:

> At the opening of the summer he appeared with a small following in the wilds of Plynlimmon and there, in a remote mountain glen, signally defeated on the banks of the river Hyddgen, a large force which had been gathered in West Wales.

Where did the idea of a conflict on the banks of the Afon Hyddgen originate? Unfortunately, Lloyd has become such a significant authority on the Glyndŵr revolt that most other modern writers have followed his lead.

Skidmore (1978) had Glyndŵr and his men "…camped in a mountain glen in the Hyddgen valley…when the Flemings burst in upon them…the Fleming army ringed the rim of the glen and their downward charge gave them a formidable advantage over the Welsh, forced to fight uphill."

Richard Sale, in the first definitive guide to the newly established Glyndŵr's Way, *Owain Glyndŵr's Way* (1992), states that:

> The Flemings had superiority in numbers, they had the element of surprise in their favour and the benefit of terrain, as they poured downhill into the valley and onto the trapped Welshmen.

Here is a complete reversal of the situation described by Gruffydd Hiraethog, Ellis and others, where the accounts clearly indicate a hilltop engagement. In addition, these (and other) modern writers suggest a short, sharp skirmish, rather than the lengthy engagement described by the older writers. All writers on Glyndŵr since Lloyd, if they mention the Battle of Hyddgen, ascribe to it a valley location. Clearly the idea of the invading force creeping unsuspected upon the rebel camp in a remote mountain valley and then charging downhill at them has appeal, even if it is incorrect. However, the Hyddgen valley is certainly no "mountain glen". It is a wide and marshy valley between low hills. Few areas of lowland in the valley would have been suitable for an encampment and shelter would have been (as it is now) singularly lacking. Therefore, the image of Flemings bursting out from behind rocky outcrops or leaping down steep hillsides can, I suggest, be discounted. Hyddgen is not that kind of site and wouldn't have been in 1401 either.

Having looked at the written accounts of the battle, it is clear that the earliest written sources give a hilltop location for the engagement but that writers over the last 70 years have turned things around, locating the battle down in the Hyddgen valley. One reason may have been the location of the "Covenant Stones of Owain Glyndŵr" (Cerrig Cyfammod Owain Glyndŵr), large unhewn calcite blocks set up alongside the Afon Hyddgen. It is tempting to regard the Covenant Stones as representative of the battle site, as well as being commemorative, rather enigmatically, of the place where, according to local tradition, "Owain Glyndŵr held parley and made his covenant." On the first occasion that I visited the Hyddgen Valley it was very tempting to visualise the battle as taking place on the flat shelf of land to the west of the Afon Hyddgen. I now firmly believe that such an assumption is false.

Since written sources, such as they are, indicate Mynydd Hyddgen as the site of the battle, what can be learned from oral sources? Cledwyn Fychan's work on the oral traditions of the Hyddgen shepherds, has led him to believe that Siambr Trawsfynydd was the site of the rebel camp. Local oral tradition certainly points to a hilltop battle site, although the area of Esgair y Ffordd, the (currently) forested ridge at the north-east end of the Hyddgen valley, seems the favoured site, rather than Mynydd Hyddgen itself. Esgair y Ffordd is close to Siambr Trawsfynydd and seems a logical site for the battle if Glyndŵr was surprised by the invading force. Furthermore, we should not necessarily interpret "Mynydd Hyddgen" to mean the actual summit currently crowned by the two huge cairns named "Carn Gwilym" on the Ordnance Survey map. The term "Pumlumon" can be taken to refer to the whole Pumlumon upland area. Similarly, "Mynydd Hyddgen" could refer to all the high land on the east and north-east of the Hyddgen valley. This would tie a battle site at Esgair y Ffordd to the early written accounts. However, if we accept the idea of a lengthy siege-like engagement, Esgair y Ffordd is a much less likely site than Mynydd Hyddgen. It is a smooth rounded ridge, without a prominent defensible summit and it is difficult to see how a small rebel band could have held out here against a force three times larger.

We can never be completely certain about the site of the Battle of Hyddgen, but, having examined what evidence exists, my conclusion is that it took place on the summit of Mynydd Hyddgen.

The Battle of Hyddgen: the preamble

It is time now to come out from the sheltering ambiguity of the various sources of information about the Battle of Hyddgen and to make some assertions about what did take place. Certainty is impossible, but it is my belief that the events of the early summer of 1401, in the northern part of the Pumlumon uplands, were broadly as follows.

During the month of May 1401, Owain Glyndŵr realised that he needed to shift the focus of the revolt southwards. English Royal power in North Wales was implacable and growing; the opposition of Hotspur, Justiciar of North Wales, had increasingly made Glyndŵr's position in the North untenable. Even before Hotspur and Charlton's victories over Welsh rebel forces at the end of May, it is likely that an advance force went south into the Pumlumon uplands to establish a base camp for offensive operations in Mid and South Wales and that Glyndŵr's main group of followers joined them in early June.

Gruffydd Hiraethog's "120 reckless men and robbers" had, by the 1851 Archaeologia Cambrensis account, become, "a detachment of his army, consisting of 120 men at arms." Are we therefore to visualise a guerrilla band or an organised force of 480 (on the authority of Pennant) consisting of 360 archers and 120 swordsmen? I suspect that the truth lies between the two extremes. Certainly, the successes to date of Glyndŵr's men were those of a guerrilla band rather than of an organised army. However, he had begun to realise that some more formalised military organisation was necessary to confront disciplined English forces.

Although the Welsh rebel band in Pumlumon was still very much a guerrilla force, there may have been some specialisation within its numbers, with most men concentrating on archery and others prepared to fight as foot soldiers, with the sword as their main weapon. In addition, a range of other weapons would have been used, including axes, pikes and billhooks.

The base already set up in May 1401 for Glyndŵr's force by his advance guard was probably at Siambr Trawsfynydd, in the north of the Pumlumon area and in close contact with the fertile lowlands of the Dyfi valley, where Glyndŵr undoubtedly had supporters. It is possible that other temporary camps were established in other parts of the Pumlumon uplands over the next few weeks, but the Siambr was well hidden and provided some shelter from the weather, at least for Glyndŵr himself and other rebel leaders. Nearby, the main rebel force of around 500 or so men, perhaps also with a variety of camp followers, was able to set up shelters alongside the stream. Horses and ponies may have been grazed nearby during the day but removed to the safer surroundings of caves or overhanging cliffs north of the Siambr (Y Stablau) at nightfall or when danger threatened. It is very likely that a number of outposts were established to provide advance warning of any movement by English or pro-Crown forces. A post on Pumlumon Fawr itself is likely, and a post on the top of Mynydd Hyddgen, the 1,850 foot high summit south-west of Siambr Trawsfynydd, commanding a superb view down the Rheidol valley. This was possibly even better as a viewpoint than Pumlumon Fawr, since the latter is often shrouded in low cloud.

Life in the rebel camp would have been exciting, as raiding parties returned with loot and stories of their successes, but, unless the summer of 1401 was an unusual one, it would also have been wet and cold. The weather in the Pumlumon area is often poor and there is enough evidence, from the frequent accounts later in the Glyndŵr Revolt of

English armies worn down by constant heavy rainfall, to suggest that unseasonal, wet and stormy conditions prevailed in the early years of the fifteenth century.

In late May and early June 1401, Glyndŵr's reinvigorated rebel force launched a devastating series of raids from their new, secure base in the Pumlumon uplands. These raids went east, south-east and, most tellingly, south-west. Raiding parties returned with loot from farms and churches, perhaps with some hostages, and, most likely, with sheep and cattle driven off from plundered farms and estates. These very successes to a certain extent increased the vulnerability of Glyndŵr's force in Pumlumon. The traditional view of a tiny band of hunted outlaws sheltering in a remote mountain valley may be far from the truth. Instead, we should visualise an increasingly sophisticated rebel military operation, irregular in nature, but organised to spread terror and seek plunder throughout the central and southern parts of Wales. It was the success of this campaign that shook Parliament in London, while its effect upon the Flemish communities of the south-west was critical for the next stage of the Revolt. So the successful warbands ranged far and wide, the Pumlumon valleys began to fill with captured sheep and cattle and the location of Glyndŵr's base became much less easy to conceal.

The organised response to the rebels came from the Anglo-Flemish community of south-west Wales. Stung by the depradations of Glyndŵr's raiding parties, a strong force was assembled and no less than 1,500 men marched north to eliminate the threat to the Anglo-Flemish settlers. The force seems to have been composed of men from Pembrokeshire, south Cardiganshire and even the coastal regions between Carmarthen and the Gower. We have no idea who led it, nor whether it was augmented by additional Crown troops. It was undoubtedly a formidable force. The Flemish settlers in the southern part of Pembrokeshire had originally been protected by Flemish mercenary troops from the Plantagenet Kings and the army which set out to settle with Glyndŵr must have included descendents of these mercenaries. A hard bitten and competent military force must be visualised, well equipped, determined to avenge the attacks on their homes and to remove the threat of Welsh revolt permanently.

If we apply the "men at arms" rule to the size of the Anglo-Flemish army, it may have comprised about 1,100 archers and 400 foot soldiers. The foot soldiers would not have been identified by any particular uniform. They are likely to have worn homespun short jackets and leggings, perhaps with leather jerkins or quilted jackets (gambesons) for added protection. Slightly better off individuals may have sported light scale armour coats. Headwear varied, but many would have worn broad–rimmed "kettle hats" or iron skull caps laced under the chin. Variations to this theme included armour or accoutrements stolen from the corpses of wealthy knights in battle. Spears of varying length were popular weapons and English troops often sported billhooks, with a hook to pull down a horseman and a point for stabbing. Shafted axes may also have been used. Both archers and foot soldiers carried small wooden shields, called bucklers, used for parrying enemy blows in close combat.

The archers in the Anglo-Flemish force were, in a sense, the elite troops. The longbow had been used with devastating effect by the English Kings since Edward I and, ironically, the best bowmen, were originally Welsh. An Anglo-Flemish bowman may have worn a quilted jerkin over a homespun shirt, a light helmet and a leather belt, from which hung a light sword. He would have carried his bow unstrung and sheathed in a canvas sleeve. It is also possible that there were crossbowmen in the Anglo-Flemish force. The crossbow was a formidable weapon, capable, by the start of the fifteenth century, of hitting a target 200 yards distant. Its drawback, however, was its slow rate of fire. Compared to a longbowman's ten arrows per minute, the crossbowman could, at best, manage three bolts, or quarrels, per minute, and the reloading process was cumbersome, leaving the crossbowman dangerously exposed between shots. The longbow remained the prime weapon. Christopher Rothero, in *The Scottish and Welsh Wars* (1984), comments that:

> ...a massed formation of English longbowmen could lay down a devastating arrow-storm, which became ever more effective as the range closed. At anything approaching hand-to-hand range, the effect on a closely packed mess would have been little less lethal than a machine gun.

This was the nature of the force which set out during June 1401 to attack Glyndŵr in his Pumlumon stronghold. On past experience, Glyndŵr's small band of 500 rebel fighters stood little chance against such an onslaught.

The arrival of the Anglo-Flemish troops in the Pumlumon area may have been unexpected, but there is no reason to believe that Glyndŵr was caught completely unprepared. Outposts were probably maintained on high points to provide advance warning. However, it seems that the Anglo-Flemish force was cautious in its approach and that some element of surprise was achieved. There were no doubt those who were prepared to sell information on the whereabouts of the rebel camp to the invaders, or possibly escaped hostages from rebel raids who were only too happy to get their own back upon Glyndŵr by helping the Crown forces.

The *Archaeologia Cambrensis* account of the battle suggests that:

> The approach of the Flemings from the south to surprise Owain was probably along the valley of the Rheidol, which, at its first descent from the hills, inclines to a southerly direction, and would thus far be their guide, till at the well known Falls of the Devil's Bridge, it meets with the Mynach and takes a westerly course to the sea. From the falls ...to the Teifi is but a

few miles distance, whence that river might be their route from the borders of Pembrokeshire.

This seems a logical route, but local oral tradition suggests that part of the invading force proceeded north to bypass the uplands and then marched up the (upper) Hengwm valley to attack Glyndŵr from a totally unexpected direction. Cledwyn Fychan believes the Anglo-Flemish troops may have made good use of ridges rather than valley bottoms, to avoid wet and marshy areas. Whatever the detail of the advance, which will probably never be known, there is no doubt that the rapid advance of such a strong, organised force and its descent upon the rebels in the Pumlumon uplands, possibly from two directions at the same time, was a substantial military feat which might easily have put an end to the Glyndŵr Revolt. Perhaps Glyndŵr's intelligence sources were too embryonic to give warning of the new threat, or perhaps the rebels had become over-confident after their recent successes. In either event, the future of the whole rebel enterprise was now at stake.

The Battle of Hyddgen: an account of the battle

The 500 or so men whom Glyndŵr commanded were probably equipped and attired very similarly to the troops in the Anglo-Flemish force. Once again, the archers were a significant element. It is likely that all were longbowmen, experienced and seasoned men, used to a hard outdoor life and, more recently, skilled in the specifics of guerrilla warfare: swift descents upon outposts and strongholds, diversionary attacks upon large and slow–moving bodies of troops. Many were probably mounted upon sturdy hill ponies.

How should Owain Glyndŵr himself be imagined? There are traditions about him mounted upon a destrier, or warhorse, Llwyd-y-Bacsie, and his harness and accoutrements would probably have been similar to those of many other early fifteenth century nobles. He may have worn a "pot helm", a metal helmet enclosing the whole head, and body plate armour. Glyndŵr's mount was probably enveloped in a cloth trapper, carrying his coat of arms. We can, of course, have no way of knowing whether Glyndŵr fought the Battle of Hyddgen on horseback or on foot. Certainly, there are strong local traditions about a mounted Glyndŵr raising his golden dragon standard on the summit of Pumlumon Fawr, but I suspect that this was after the victory was won.

The date of the Battle of Hyddgen cannot be determined with any accuracy. There is simply too little definitive source material. I suggest that the battle did not take place before the middle of June. This rough timescale would permit the arrival of the main rebel force in Pumlumon after they had quit North Wales (probably the very beginning of June) and give time for several days of sustained raiding from the Pumlumon base. It would also allow for the rapid response of the Anglo-Flemish community in the south-west and the forced march north to confront Glyndŵr. Tentatively let us place the battle in the third week of June, 1401.

My belief is that the rapidity of the Anglo-Flemish advance, converging from the south-west and from the north at the same time, caused Glyndŵr problems, although his scouts and outposts would have reported the advance in time for some evasive action. The invading force advancing up the Hengwm valley from the north may well have aimed to attack the rebel camp in Siambr Trawsfynydd. However, the Welsh rebel force was well used to rapid movement across difficult ground. They probably had ample time to evacuate the Siambr and move south-westwards along the marshy moorland shoulder of Ochr Llygnant to the prominent and defensible summit plateau of Mynydd Hyddgen. Meanwhile, the main body of the Anglo-Flemish army was advancing up the Rheidol, or possibly along the ridge to the east of that river. If the military intelligence of the invaders was really as good as it seems to have been, the main force may have perhaps been around 1,000 men, leaving 500 or so to take the northern route to surprise Glyndŵr from an unexpected direction.

Let us imagine the smaller Anglo-Flemish force marching up towards the Siambr, only to find, on arrival, that the rebel camp was empty. In their frustration, they probably torched the simple huts and shelters which they found there, killed any stragglers or wounded rebels left behind, seized any abandoned provisions or weapons, and then turned towards the Hyddgen valley to meet up with the main force advancing up from the Rheidol.

Meanwhile, Glyndŵr and his 500 followers had set up their defensive position on Carn, or Mynydd Hyddgen, on the east side of the Hyddgen valley. Mynydd Hyddgen has a long western ridge, dropping down towards the Afon Hyddgen, easily climbed, although steep in places. On its north side, the Nant y Garn flows down the hillside. On the north-west side of the summit, an area of irregular rocky outcrops breaks up the tussocky grass of the open hillside. The actual summit plateau is roughly circular in shape, dropping on all sides. There is a marshy area just to the west of the summit plateau, while, to the east and south-east, great peat bogs stretch away across the moorland. Mynydd Hyddgen is today easily recognisable from afar by reason of its two huge stone cairns, but these have nothing to do with the battle, probably having been constructed by shepherds to aid direction–finding in mist.

I suggest that the Battle of Hyddgen was a lengthy engagement, divided into three phases. The first saw the Anglo-Flemish force arrive at the foot of Mynydd Hyddgen and begin to ascend the lower slopes. Since they had the advantage of numbers, they could have assaulted the summit from a number of directions. The approach from south-east or east was impractical, owing to the extremely boggy terrain here. Assaults up the length of the western spur ridge of Mynydd Hyddgen, up both steeper sides of that ridge, up the Nant y Garn and, possibly, along the higher ground from the north, are all likely. The defenders had the advantage of the high ground and their archers could beat off these attacks by firing downwards. The Anglo-Flemish troops were not massed in a body and the defenders would have had to pick them off individually. At the same time, the invading force would have employed its own longbowmen to some effect, although the range was probably too great for significant damage. So, round one of the Battle of Hyddgen resulted, I suspect, in a stand off. The Anglo-Flemish side perhaps realised that they really only had to sit and wait, while the Welsh defenders of the hilltop, no doubt elated to have beaten off so superior a force, began to worry whether their hastily gathered supplies would stand a long siege.

The second phase of the battle may have lasted for several days. The

Hyddgen Valley and the surrounding area

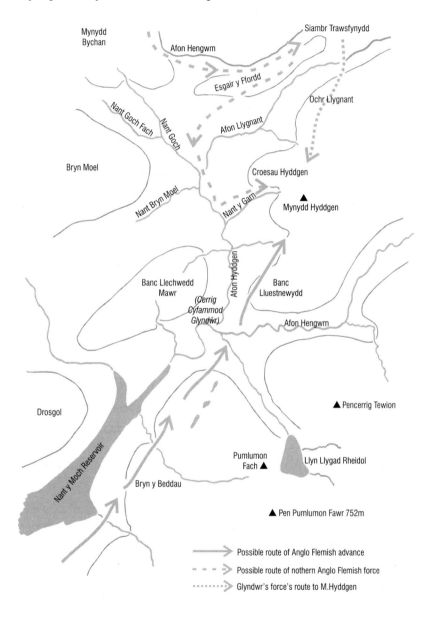

Mynydd Bychan

Afon Hengwm

Siambr Trawsfynydd

Esgair y Ffordd

Ochr Llygnant

Nant Goch Fach

Nant Goch

Afon Llygnant

Bryn Moel

Croesau Hyddgen

Nant Bryn Moel

Nant y Garn

Mynydd Hyddgen ▲

Afon Hyddgen

Banc Llechwedd Mawr

(Cerrig Cyfammod Glyndŵr)

Banc Lluestnewydd

Afon Hengwm

Pencerrig Tewion ▲

Drosgol

Nant y Moch Reservoir

Pumlumon Fach ▲

Llyn Llygad Rheidol

Bryn y Beddau

▲ Pen Pumlumon Fawr 752m

Possible route of Anglo Flemish advance

Possible route of nothern Anglo Flemish force

Glyndwr's force's route to M.Hyddgen

Anglo-Flemish troops organised themselves into a besieging force and settled down to wait for the defenders to weaken through lack of food, before making a final assault on the hilltop. They tightened the noose around the hill and probably launched regular arrow strikes onto the defenders, perhaps creeping close to the rebel stronghold under cover of darkness so that the range was substantially reduced. These tactics kept up the pressure on the defenders, by killing or wounding individuals on the hilltop and by necessitating a continuous state of alarm. The rebel band could not be sure when the next arrow strike might come. Over a number of days, supplies of food held by the defenders began to run out. There was no chance of obtaining more and hunger gripped them. One tradition has Glyndŵr marching his depleted and exhausted band round and round the hilltop, to give the impression there were large numbers of defenders.

The third phase of the battle saw the almost incredible Welsh victory over the investing force. Whatever Glyndŵr actually said to his followers, the effect of his words was electric. There was nothing to lose by a final attack on the Anglo-Flemish force. All probably believed that, with no source of further supplies, they would be so weakened that when the Anglo-Flemish force finally assaulted the hilltop they would inevitably perish. Hence the all or nothing decision to "sell lives dearly" and to try to cut through the investing force. At the same time, the Anglo-Flemish troops had probably grown a little slack and over-confident. The last thing they expected was a wild downhill charge by the defenders, whom they probably believed to be on their last legs. So, the charge, when it came, was devastating. The Welsh rebels, fighting out of pure desperation, poured downhill off the summit and charged into the surrounding force like a fury. Glyndŵr's swordsmen, for so long denied any real action in this battle, now carried the field, cutting down no fewer than 200 of the enemy. The effect was immediate. Anglo-Flemish archers and swordsmen ran in fear from this new and dreadful manifestation of Glyndŵr's magical powers. A force of under 500 starving and desperate men had routed an elite and hardened military force three times their number.

The immediate aftermath of the battle

There is no way of telling precisely what occurred after Glyndŵr's men completed their downhill charge and, fighting more from desperation than any expectation of success, snatched a brilliant victory from the jaws of almost certain defeat. The rebels' attack, perhaps concentrated only at one point in the encircling ring of troops, transmitted a shock of panic through the whole body of the Anglo-Flemish force. Perhaps, typically for Hyddgen, the weather was wet or misty, when visibility would have been reduced and the Welsh attack all the more unexpected. The renewed vigour of the Welsh defenders may also have been taken as a signal of the arrival of rebel reinforcements.

Looking once again at the main sources for comment on the nature of the victory, Gruffydd Hiraethog stated:

> ...no sooner did the English troops turn their backs in flight than 200 of them were slain.

Thomas Ellis added:

> ...they put the enemy, after sharp dispute, to confusion, and they pursued so eagerly their advantage, that they made them give ground, and in the end to fly outright, leaving two hundred of their men dead on the spot of engagement.

Finally, *Archaeologia Cambrensis* (1851) stated:

> ...they executed the command with such impetuosity, that the Flemings, thrown into confusion, took to flight in the greatest disorder, leaving two hundred of their party dead on the field of battle.

Certainly all these accounts refer to an attack coming as a surprise to the Anglo-Flemish force. They also all attest to the ferocity of the Welsh attack and hint at a panic among the defenders.

It may have been some little time before the full significance of the victory was realised by Glyndŵr's men. Since they had probably expected to sell their lives dearly, the reversal in their fortunes may have been hard to grasp. Only the sight of the remaining Anglo-Flemish troops fleeing back down the Hyddgen valley, leaving behind a large number of their comrades on the hillside, brought their victory home to the exhausted rebels. Glyndŵr could not pursue the defeated force; indeed, to attempt to do so would probably have only demonstrated how weak the rebels really were.

What would have been the actions of Glyndŵr's men following the battle? One of the first would have been to seize food and drink from the now deserted Anglo-Flemish encampment. Shortly afterwards, or even simultaneously, they would have looted the bodies of the fallen enemy, removing weapons, armour, useful articles of clothing and personal possessions. Any wounded enemy foot soldiers or archers would have been finished off with a sword stroke or dagger thrust. Any wounded aristocrats may have been taken hostage. It seems likely that Glyndŵr made no effort to bury the bodies of the Anglo-Flemish troops after they had been robbed. They were probably left naked on the hillside to rot and be picked over by crows. This was an era of cruel and violent warfare.

The bodies of fallen rebels would have been buried, while wounded men would have received whatever treatment was feasible. It has to be remembered that to be severely wounded in a medieval battle was a worse fate than being killed outright, since medical and surgical intervention was very limited and often ineffective. A man who lost a limb in battle would be hard pressed to survive the pain and loss of blood and, if he did so, faced a future of grinding poverty and hardship, since his ability to pursue a trade or occupation was severely limited.

It is likely that Glyndŵr buried the Welsh dead in the area of the battle. There are a number of local sites which point to possible burials or commemorative cairns. However, although records are held for nearly all of these sites, both in the Royal Commission for Historical Monuments in Wales' archives and in those of both the Clwyd-Powys and the Dyfed Archaeological Trusts, detail is lacking and little archaeological investigation has taken place. We must turn again to local oral traditions to provide more clues.

On Esgair y Ffordd, one of the possible sites for the battle are the remains of a cairn that could have been erected to commemorate the victory or, more likely, to act as a monument for some, if not all, of the fallen Welsh rebels. The account in *Archaeologia Cambrensis* refers to the Esgair y Ffordd site as follows:

> On Esgair y Ffordd, a mountain ridge in sight of Plynlimon, and adjoining Hyddgen, is a round earthen tumulus, which may have been the place of sepulture of those who fell in battle on this occasion, and near it is a round cairn of grey mountain stones.

A little to the west, on Moel Bychan, is another cairn. Both these cairns may have been built, perhaps in medieval times, on the site of Bronze Age barrows, and could have been raised after the Battle of Hyddgen. Further west, close to the western end of the modern Nant y Moch reservoir, is "Carn Owen" on the hilltop of Cerrig yr Hafan. This seems to have been adapted over the last hundred years to provide some shelter for sheep. There is no indication why the site is called Carn Owen, nor whether "Owen" refers to Owain Glyndŵr, although it is tempting to think so.

A rather enigmatic site can be found close to the eastern arm of the Nant y Moch reservoir, east of the Rheidol valley. This is Bryn y

Beddau, Hill of the Graves, a steep hillside below Pumlumon Fach. Although there is no evidence from excavation, the name of the site indicates a burial place and local traditions suggest that it could be the resting place for some, if not all, of the Welsh dead after the Battle of Hyddgen.

There is a story that Owain Glyndŵr rode to the summit of Pumlumon Fawr after the battle and raised there his battle flag, a golden dragon on a white field. A triumphal procession around the upland of Pumlumon is very plausable, once the Anglo-Flemish menace had been defeated.

What, then, of the so-called Covenant Stones of Owain Glyndŵr (Cerrig Cyfammod Owain Glyndŵr)? These blocks of unhewn calcite stand on the grassy shelf near the confluence of Hyddgen and Hengwm. Tradition has it that the stones mark the point where Owain Glyndŵr "held parley and made his covenant". They have been taken by some in the past to commemorate the Battle of Hyddgen, but it is unclear how Glyndŵr might have held parley with the enemy before the battle. "Held parley" might refer to a post-battle process, with Glyndŵr conceivably meeting representatives from the defeated Anglo-Flemish force, or, more likely, local leaders who had arrived to treat with the victorious rebel leader. "Made his covenant" could refer to Glyndŵr renewing his pledge to liberate Wales from the rule of the English Crown. There have been suggestions of significant symbolism in the north-south alignment of the Covenant Stones. One local tradition has them so aligned to represent Glyndŵr's concern for and claim over both North and South Wales.

All this speculation may be baseless. Another local tradition, reported by Cledwyn Fychan, has the Covenant Stones commemorating Glyndŵr's pact with Mortimer towards the end of 1402, after the Welsh victory at Bryn Glas (Pilleth) and Mortimer's subsequent imprisonment by Glyndŵr. We may never be sure about the origins of the Covenant Stones, but they are the only surviving tangible reminder of Glyndŵr's time in Pumlumon.

The longer term aftermath of the battle

Glyndŵr's victory at Hyddgen sent a signal far and wide that the rebellion was succeeding. Prior to the Battle of Hyddgen, rebel successes had been of the guerrilla, irregular, hit and run variety. Now, for the first time, a serious military force sent out in opposition to the rebels had been defeated. Support began to pour into the rebel cause from all parts of Wales.

Gruffydd Hiraethog stated:

> Owen now won great fame, and a great number of youths and fighting men from every part of Wales rose and joined him, until he had a great host at his back.

The implication here is that Glyndŵr's forces were augmented not just by opportunist adventurers, who may have rallied to the rebel cause in the expectation of glory and loot, but also hardened soldiers who may initially have been much more cautious about throwing in their lot with the rebels.

Thomas Ellis's account stated:

> This victory rendered Owain considerable renown and was the means to bring many to his side, that his number was greatly increased.

The account in *Archaeologia Cambrensis* (1851) stated:

> This gallant exploit, achieved against so great a superiority of forces, had the effect not only of extending the popularity of the Welsh chieftain among his countrymen, and of producing a

considerable accession to the number of his followers, but also of awakening the apprehension of Henry.

Bradley's 1928 account stated:

This personal feat of arms was worth five thousand men to Owain. It was all that was wanted to fill the measure of his prestige and decide every wavering Welshman in his favour.

Secure in his Pumlumon base, Glyndŵr's forces continued the plundering raids carried out before the Battle of Hyddgen. It was probably now that the massacre at New Radnor took place. Anxious to avenge the defeat at Welshpool, which had occurred at the hands of Hugh Burnell in September 1400, the rebel army marched once again to attack the town. They were defeated by the superior forces of John Charlton, but not before they had sacked and burnt Welshpool. Meanwhile, Henry IV wavered about the best course of action, all the time mindful of the shortage of money in the royal treasury to pay for military expeditions into Wales.

Skidmore, in *Owain Glyndŵr, Prince of Wales*, paints a picture of life in the rebel camp post-Hyddgen:

In the mountains, Owain was in better case. His treasury was full and, despite the reversal at Welshpool, his soldiers were in good heart. Those months in the mountains were the golden time. The meadows round his camp were thick with the cattle his men had driven from the lowlands, and the higher slopes white with flocks of sheep. Relaxed now, the blood bath over, Owain was able once again to entertain visiting poets. The Children, equally adept with the crwth and the axe, sang to the music of harps.

In the early autumn of 1401, Glyndŵr left his base in the Pumlumon uplands. The time had come to take to the field against Crown forces in Wales. Meanwhile, Henry IV issued a commission of array for an army to assemble at Worcester on 1 October. The subsequent "invasion", an armed cavalry raid in depth, penetrated South Wales as far as Carmarthen and sacked the abbey of Strata Florida near Aberystwyth. Nothing significant was achieved. Welsh guerrilla bands refused to be drawn into battle and there was no contact between Glyndŵr and the royal army. However, the effect of the depradations of the royal army upon the land of Wales was cataclysmic. The army burned and looted its way though the countryside, reducing the peasantry to starvation and ruin and building a smouldering resentment that was to fuel the continuation of the Revolt.

At first glance, it seems that the Welsh rebels were faring no better in the autumn of 1401 than they had in the previous autumn, despite their great victory at Hyddgen. However, things had changed signally in their favour. Glyndŵr, elusive as ever to the searching English troops of Henry's army, now had a sizeable force at his back and was beginning to take the initiative in terms of field operations. There would still be setbacks, but the rebels had notably increased their power and confidence at Hyddgen. Furthermore, the royal policy of chevauchée and reprisal further boosted the rebel cause, alienating from the Crown many in Wales who had, until now, preferred to remain on the sidelines in the conflict. Towards the end of 1401, Glyndŵr felt strong enough to assault Caernarfon Castle, chief royal fortress in North Wales. He did not take it, but the attempt frightened Henry IV enough to make him consider, for a short time, a negotiated peace with the rebels.

Another development at the end of 1401 was Glyndŵr's attempt to forge alliances with Scotland and Ireland, a move which, although unsuccessful, clearly placed him beyond the status of local warlord. The year 1402 saw some great rebel successes, notably the capture of Lord Grey of Ruthin and the victory at Bryn Glas (Pilleth) in June, leading to Glyndŵr's fateful alliance with Mortimer.

This is not intended to be another history of the Glyndŵr Revolt and I will go no further in narrative terms. I will, however, state once again that rebel success flowed directly from the victory at Hyddgen. The whole future of the rebel cause lay in the balance when Glyndŵr made the fateful decision to risk all in the attack upon the Anglo-Flemish troops. Without the Welsh victory at Hyddgen, there would have been no extension of the revolt and no increase in the numbers of fighting men eager to serve their own Welsh Prince. The Battle of Hyddgen deserves to be recognised as one of the decisive battles of Welsh history.

Poetry about the Battle of Hyddgen

There are few written sources about the Battle of Hyddgen, but there is some poetry relating to the battle. It is all modern, although there were doubtless many bards in the rebel camp after the battle who sang songs and composed penillion about the great success achieved by Glyndŵr's small band of warriors on Mynydd Hyddgen.

The Owain Glyndŵr Centre in Machynlleth has published two poems in a small booklet about Glyndŵr's associations with Machynlleth. The first, *The Battle of Mynydd Hyddgen,* was written by David Grugog Mason. It may have been composed at the time of the completion of the Hyddgen mural by Murray Urquhart in 1909.

THE BATTLE OF MYNYDD HYDDGEN

Night has fallen on Hyddgen
Her black wing aspread
O'er the camp of Glyndŵr, chief warrior,
The hero of all heroes;
After a day's long search
For the over-bold Flemings,
To his weary warriors
The bare mountain is a bed of down.

Night has fallen on Hyddgen
Owain's men in peaceful sleep,
But even in slumber, how ready,
The sword in each hand;
The warriors, though sleeping,
Hear the marching of feet nearby − the host
To a man is awakened, with sinews all tight,
And a terrible battle was fought.

Dawn broke upon Hyddgen,
After a night when blood ran so free,
With Owain Glyndŵr in his triumph,
His warriors loudly sing his praises;
His foes in their graves are up yonder
And the Rheidol in the valley below,
Sings the praise of our fathers so valiant,
Who kept the invaders at bay.

BRWYDR BRYN HYDDGANT

Mae'r nos wedi disgyn ar Hyddgant,
Gan ledu ei haden ddu
Dros wersyll Glyndŵr y pendragon
Prif arwr yr arwyr fu;
'Rôl dyddgwaith o wibio mewn ymchwil
I lwybriad y Fleming hy'
Mae noethder y mynydd i'w filwyr
Lluddedig, fel gwely plu.

Mae'r nos wedi disgyn ar Hyddgant –
Gwŷr Owain gânt hun ddi-ffraw –
Ond tra yn eu cwsg, mor effro
Y cleddyf sydd yn y llaw;
Mor denau yw clust y lleuddwr –
Clyw sangdrwst! – a dacw'r llu
Yn deffro – a deffry pob gewyn,
A chyfranc ofnadwy fu.

Disgynnodd y wawrddydd ar Hyddgant
'Rôl noson y waedlyd drin
A chafodd Glyndŵr yn orchfygwr,
A'i ddewrion yn moli ei rin;
Fry acw ceir beddi'r gelynion,
A'r Rheidol fyth gan islaw
Arwyrain ein tadau glew galon
Gadwasant y gelyn draw.

The second poem published by the Owain Glyndŵr Centre is entitled *Glyndŵr's Victory* and was written by Meirwen Hughes, a native of Aberhosan, near Machynlleth.

GLYNDŴR'S VICTORY

And did he place his crown
On a shelf deep in the rock
Until the bright dawn comes
When the Dragon again
Flies over the hills
To loudly proclaim

Our victory gained
After battle so bitter.

Yes, Glyndŵr clothed in dignity
These ancient hills;
Oh! To see above the mists
Again his banner gold and white.
No, his was no mortal clay,
His spirit, borne on the wind,
Calls all to a new awakening.
As in days of yore.

BUDDIGOLIAETH GLYNDŴR

A adawodd ef ei goron
Ar ryw astell yn y Graig
Hyd nes gwawria'r bore disglair,
Pan y gwelir eto'r Ddraig,
Yn cyhwfan uwch y bryniau
I gyhoeddi gyda grym
Ennill gyflawn fuddugoliaeth
Wedi'r siom a'r brwydro llym.

Do, fe roddodd Owain urddas
Ar yr hen gopaon hyn,
O na welen uwch y niwloedd
Eto'r faner aur a gwyn;
Na, nid priddyn oedd ei ddeunydd
Mae ei ysbryd yn y gwynt
Yn cyniwair deffroadau
Megis yn y dyddiau gynt.

A third poem about Hyddgen is reproduced here. It was written by the great Welsh poet R S Thomas and is entitled simply *Hyddgen*.

HYDDGEN

The place, Hyddgen;
The time, the fifth
Century since Glyndŵr
Was here with his men
He beat the English.
Does it matter now
In the rain? The English
Don't want to come;
Summer country.
The Welsh too:
A barren victory.
Look at those sheep
On such small bones
The best mutton.
But not for him,
The hireling shepherd.
History goes on;
On the rock the lichen
Records it: no mention
Of them, of us.

Visiting Hyddgen and associated sites today

Owain Glyndŵr Centre, Machynlleth and the Hyddgen Murals

Anyone who is keen to visit the site of the battle and some of the other features in and around the Hyddgen valley would do well to start in Machynlleth, the town most associated with Owain Glyndŵr and the site of his first Parliament in 1404. The Owain Glyndŵr Centre in Maengwyn Street is well worth a visit, to view the ancient building, which, although not the actual site of Glyndŵr's Parliament, is a rare example of a late medieval Welsh town house, and to seek out the Hyddgen murals. There are four large murals, high up on an interior wall of the Reading Room in the "Parliament House". The two central murals depict Glyndŵr's forces besieging a castle, but it is the ones on the far right and far left that will be of particular interest to those who seek more information about the Battle of Hyddgen.

The murals were painted by Murray Urquhart in 1909, ready for the opening of the Owain Glyndŵr Institute in February 1912. The restoration of the Old Parliament House and two adjoining cottages, and the creation of a centre to commemorate the life of Owain Glyndŵr as well as to provide accommodation for Machynlleth Town Council, was funded by David Davies of Llandinam. The murals were designed to depict striking incidents in Glyndŵr's career and the Battle of

Hyddgen was seen as highly significant. The right of the two Hyddgen murals depicts Glyndŵr speaking to his men on the hilltop, while the left shows him encouraging the downward assault upon the encircling Anglo-Flemish force.

HYDDGEN MONUMENT, NANT Y MOCH RESERVOIR (OS GRID REFRENCE 862756)

In 1977, Gwynfor Evans unveiled a monument to Glyndŵr's victory at Hyddgen. The memorial stone, set in a stone cairn, is to be found at the eastern end of the Nant y Moch dam and reads:

> This cairn was built to commemorate Owain Glyndŵr, who raised his standard on the River Hyddgen in May 1401. The ensuing battle resulted in a victory for the Welsh against the crown forces of Henry IV.

SITES TO VISIT IN THE HYDDGEN AREA:

Most sites associated with the battle can be visited, although all demand stout walking boots, since cross country walking is necessary. I will list the main sites in this section, with their OS grid references, and then suggest three enjoyable walking routes which could be followed by those interested in the battle.

Mynydd Hyddgen or Carn Gwilym (909792) itself is obviously the key spot to visit. It can be reached fairly easily from the main track down the Hyddgen valley. The two immense cairns on the summit can be seen from a considerable distance. The view from the summit of Mynydd Hyddgen on a clear day towards Nant y Moch is excellent.

Siambr Trawsfynydd (929794) is easily reached by forestry track or by a peat bog trudge across Ochr Llygnant from Mynydd Hyddgen. The construction of a forestry road destroyed the Siambr itself, but the lower reaches of the riverside glen, where Glyndŵr may have camped before the Battle of Hyddgen, can still be visited. Be prepared for long grass, tussocks and marshy spots.

Esgair y Ffordd (923792) is now covered with forestry plantations, but the remains of the cairn can be seen, alongside the track which goes over the ridge.

Mynydd Bychan (923775) is deep in the forestry and not particularly worth the trouble of visiting.

Carn Owen (883733) is a long way from the other sites mentioned, although, if you have a car, a pleasant meandering drive along the southern and western shores of the Nant y Moch reservoir will bring you near.

Bryn y Beddau (875773) is worth the short detour from the Nant y Moch – Maesnant road, although there is absolutely nothing to see, apart from the view over the reservoir.

Owain Glyndŵr's Covenant Stones (897783) are the only tangible remains from Glyndŵr's time in Pumlumon. Marked clearly on OS maps ("Standing Stones" on the 1:50000 sheet, "Cerrig Cyfammod Glyndŵr" on the 1:25000 and larger sheets), these rather unimpressive stones can be easily viewed from the Hyddgen valley track or examined more closely by fording the Afon Hyddgen, which is usually deeper than it appears!

Three walks in the Hyddgen area

Walk 1 Starting at Nant y Moch Dam (10 miles), or starting at Maesnant (7 miles)

This is the easiest route in to the Hyddgen area. It is very largely on tracks and starts on a tarmac road.

Start at the Hyddgen Monument at the Nant y Moch Dam and walk in a north-easterly direction along the tarmac road which skirts the eastern arm of Nant y Moch reservoir. The walk could be started, if preferred, where the tarmac road ends at Maesnant; there are one or two suitable places nearby to leave a car. (Deviate at this point to climb the slopes of Bryn y Beddau if you wish). Beyond Maesnant, the direction is still north-easterly, following a rough track, very muddy in wet weather, until the ruined farm buildings near the Hyddgen/ Hengwm confluence are reached. There is a footbridge over the Hengwm (892784), which you can reach via a rough, very muddy path. Once across the footbridge, strike west until you gain the broad track which runs northwards through the Hyddgen valley. (It is possible to ford the Hengwm and avoid the detour for the footbridge, but the water is often deep.)

From the Hyddgen track you can see the Covenant Stones across the Afon Hyddgen, which is now on your left. Walk up the track until it veers slightly to the west and you will see a distinctive rounded hillock between the track and the river. This is the point to turn east and ascend Mynydd Hyddgen, probably by way of the stream, Nant y Garn,

SUGGESTED WALKS IN THE HYDDGEN AREA
Based on OS Landranger
Sheet 135 (1:50000)

although a direct line straight up the nose of the western ridge is easy enough. It is worth allowing some time to examine the hilltop of Mynydd Hyddgen, take in the views, (on a fine day), and speculate about the battle which probably took place here.

If you now wish to visit Siambr Trawsfynydd, there is a choice of routes. Those who relish a direct line across moorland tussocks and peat bogs could head north-east from Mynydd Hyddgen along Ochr Llygnant, drop into the valley of the Llygnant, climb up the other side and enter the forestry plantations at 923794, then follow a track north to the Siambr. Alternatively, regain the main Hyddgen track by descending Mynydd Hyddgen the way you climbed it and follow the track north. Pass the left turn down to the Hyddgen shearing sheds and continue to the head of the Hyddgen valley, enter the forestry plantations at 936781 and then proceed downhill on a good forestry track until you reach a junction with a track on the right at 924783. Here, you can turn east and head for the Siambr via the top of Esgair y Ffordd, passing en route the remains of the cairn at 923792.

The route from Nant y Moch Dam, taking in Mynydd Hyddgen and making a circuit via Ochr Llygnant to Siambr Trawsfynydd, then returning via Esgair y Ffordd and the upper Hyddgen valley, is about **10 miles** in length. If you start from Maesnant, the distance is reduced to about **7 miles**. Should you start from Maesnant and visit Mynydd Hyddgen only, this becomes an easy walk of only about **4 miles**.

Walk 2 Starting at Glaslyn Nature Reserve (11 miles)

This walk is definitely only for those with good outdoor gear and strong waterproof boots. It is not recommended unless the weather is dry and reasonably clear, as it can be a depressing slog in grey or wet weather conditions. The Hengwm valley section is likely to be boggy in many places but most of the rest of the route is on good tracks.

There is a parking spot at Glaslyn Nature Reserve (943829), which is reached by driving down a rough but passable track south from the Machynlleth to Llanidloes "mountain road". Glaslyn is a pleasant spot on a clear day, but seems grey and uninviting when the weather is wet. Leave the lake to your right and head south-west on the broad track leading to Bugeilyn. You climb a small hill south of Glaslyn and then drop sharply down towards the ruined farm at Bugeilyn.

Just past the sheds on your right (929822), and before you reach the old farm building, take the right fork and climb briefly north-westwards above the upper of the two Bugeilyn lakes. Follow the track westward, past the small dam at the north end of the lake (930818) and then across the barren moorland. This is a good track and there is no danger of missing the route, but the views are generally fairly monotonous. Occasional glimpses of the lowlands to the north relieve the prospect a little. After a mile, the track descends towards forestry plantations. The forestry is entered at a gate at 924794 and you should turn right to reach Siambr Trawsfynydd.

After visiting the remains of the Siambr, retrace your steps southwards for about a quarter of a mile, then turn west to take the well-defined track over Esgair y Ffordd. In just under a mile, turn left (south) onto the forestry road which climbs southwards to the top of the Hyddgen valley. Follow this track through the valley, deviating eastwards to climb Mynydd Hyddgen if you wish.

Your way back to Glaslyn can, in theory, be shortened by taking a direct south-easterly line from the bottom of Mynydd Hyddgen across the slopes of Banc Lluestnewydd to reach the Hengwm valley at (approximately) 895797. However, this route is likely to be slow going, on very rough and uneven terrain, so you might find it easier to continue down the track to the bottom of the Hyddgen valley and then turn east to follow the Hengwm. Stay on the north side of the Afon Hengwm.

There is a rough path of sorts, but it occasionally disappears into bogs or becomes so faint that you have no option but to follow the general direction of the river. After some 2.5 miles, either head north-west over a hill (925814) or follow a track which now appears and skirts the west shore of Bugeilyn. At 921826 you cross the causeway between the two lakes and climb slightly to the ruined farm of Bugeilyn, then retrace your original route back to Glaslyn.

The whole circuit, allowing for a detour to Siambr Trawsfynydd and another to climb Mynydd Hyddgen, is about **11 miles**.

Walk 3 Starting at Cwmrhaiadr (9 miles)

This is one of the nicest ways to visit Hyddgen. The walking is on a mixture of tracks and moorland paths. (These may be indistinct in places and the walk is not particularly advisable, or enjoyable, in poor weather conditions.) It is good to walk over the hills and then descend into the Hyddgen valley; there is a good view of Mynydd Hyddgen ahead as you do so.

Leave a car at Cwmrhaiadr, which is at the end of the lane from Glaspwll, about 3 miles from Machynlleth. Climb steadily south-eastwards up a track which enters forestry plantations at 955767. Continue on the track, now more of a path, as it twists through the forest, changing its direction to south-westwards and finally emerging onto open hillside at 947771. Follow the path generally southwards, with good views to the east across the huge forested valley of the (northern) Hengwm. At 939765, take the track which heads south over Bwlch Hyddgen and continue south for nearly 2 miles. To the left, soon after the start of this track, are the cliffs of Criegiau Bwlch Hyddgen, beneath which, tradition has it, Glyndŵr stabled his horses.

The walk over the open moorland is a pleasant one, with good views ahead to Pumlumon Fawr, to the left over the forested Hengwm basin, and, to the right, towards Llyn Penrheadr. Do not be tempted to divert east into the forestry but continue southwards until, at about 916767, the track zigzags down a steeper hillside. It then makes a circuit of Bryn Moel before dropping down into the Hyddgen valley and heading due east for the Hyddgen shearing sheds at 909779. If you wish to climb Mynydd Hyddgen, follow the track across the Afon Hyddgen until it reaches the main north–south track through the Hyddgen valley, then turn right and, soon afterwards, ascend the slopes of Mynydd Hyddgen.

There are a number of interesting possibilities for a return that can be planned using a 1:25000 OS map, but this walk could be completed quite happily by simply retracing your outward route. The views northwards as you approach the forestry beyond Bwlch Hyddgen are fine and full of interest.

If you walk out from Cwmrhaiadr to Mynydd Hyddgen and return by the same route, the walk is about **9 miles**. A circuit to take in Siambr Trawsfynydd, after visiting Mynydd Hyddgen, and returning via Esgair y Ffordd and the north side of Mynydd Bychan would add interest and an additional 1-2 miles, to make an overall walk of about **11 miles**.

Mynydd Hyddgen from the north

Carn Gwilym: the two huge cairns on Mynydd Hyddgen   79

View from slopes of Mynydd Hyddgen

Siambr Trawsfynydd

Remains of cairn on Esgair y Ffordd

REFERENCES

Owen Glendower, Sir J E Lloyd, Llanerch 1996 (1931)

Owain Glyndŵr Prince of Wales, Ian Skidmore, Christopher Davies 1996

Owain Glyndŵr and the War of Independence in the Welsh Borders, Geoffrey Hodges, Logaston Press 1995

Owain Glyndŵr 1400-2000, National Library of Wales 2000

In Search of Owain Glyndŵr, Chris Barber, Blorenge Books 1998

The Revolt of Owain Glyndŵr, R R Davies, Oxford University Press 1997

Owain Glyndŵr, Glanmor Williams, University of Wales Press 1993

National Redeemer: Owain Glyndŵr in Welsh Tradition, Elissa Henken, University of Wales Press 1996

Figures in a Landscape, Michael Senior, Carreg Gwalch 1997

The Age of Conquest, R R Davies, Oxford University Press 1991

A Machynlleth Triad, Jan Morris, Penguin 1993

When Was Wales? Gwyn Williams, Penguin 1991

The Matter of Wales, Jan Morris, Penguin 1986

Land of My Fathers, Gwynfor Evans, Y Lolfa 1992

Medieval Wales, AD Carr, Macmillan 1995

The Scottish and Welsh Wars 1250-1400 (Men at Arms Series),
    Christopher Rothero, Osprey 1999

Guide to Welsh Wales, Ralph Maud, Y Lolfa 1994

Owain Glyndŵr and his Associations with Machynlleth, Owain Glyndŵr
Centre, Undated

Owain Glyndŵr Tywysog Cymru, Owain Glyndŵr Centre, Undated

Wild Wales, George Borrow, Collins 1962

£6.95
ISBN: 0 86243 515 3

Welsh History
A masterful history of the Welsh nation by the most distinguished
Welsh politician of the twentieth century; 500 pages.

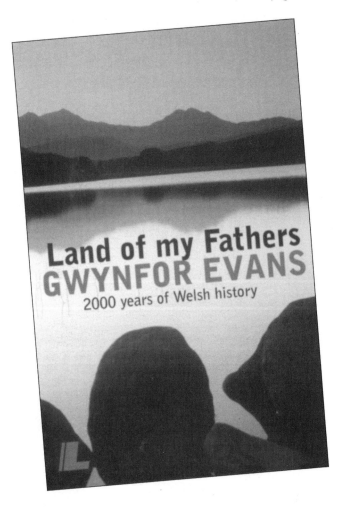

£12.95
ISBN: 0 86243 265 0

For a full list of our publications
both in English and Welsh, ask for
your free copy of our new,
full-colour, 40-page Catalogue.
Alternatively, just surf into our
website at:
www.ylolfa.com

Talybont Ceredigion Cymru/Wales SY24 5AP
ffôn 0044 (0)1970 832 304 *ffacs* 832 782 *isdn* 832 813
e-bost ylolfa@ylolfa.com *y we* www.ylolfa.com